Agents of Integration
Understanding Transfer as a Rhetorical Act

Rebecca S. Nowacek

Southern Illinois University Press
Carbondale and Edwardsville

Ratcliffe—and for their generosity of time and spirit. Each one of them read multiple drafts, offering encouragement and excellent advice at every stage. Dana Prodoehl coded hundreds of pages of transcripts, John Su read chapter 2 at a critical moment and helped me articulate its central argument, John Curran delivered much-needed pep talks, and Amy Blair offered encouragement and a crucial reading of the full manuscript. Thanks, too, to Aesha Adams-Roberts, Alice Gillam, Heather Hathaway, Chris Krueger, and Tim Machan, as well as Amy Kaboskey, Renee Anderson, and the entire staff of the truly fantastic Marquette University Childcare Center.

I'm grateful to David Russell for a pivotal conversation early in the life of this project and to CCCC Studies in Writing & Rhetoric reviewers Anis Bawarshi and Linda Adler-Kassner, who offered feedback that heartened and challenged and helped me tremendously. It has been my great pleasure to work with Joe Harris throughout this process: he has been encouraging, rigorous, and remarkably able to predict and allay the worries of a first-time author. Sincere thanks also to Karl Kageff, Kristine Priddy, Wayne Larsen, Barb Martin, and Hannah New at Southern Illinois University Press, copy editor Mary Lou Kowaleski, and Keith Wilhite at Duke University.

As a member of the Carnegie Foundation's 2005–6 cohort of CASTL scholars, I was privileged to explore the puzzle of integrative learning with colleagues from across the country and the disciplines. My special thanks to Pat Hutchings and all the "kangaroos," to Carmen Werder and Howard Tinberg for breakfasts, to Jack Mino for his feedback on a midstage draft, to Mike Burke for being my "critical friend," and to Jeff Bernstein and Michael Smith for reading drafts, sharing poems, and teaching me to love baseball.

And most of all, thanks to my family—to the Schoenikes, Schwengels, Schreckengosts, and Nowaceks. My three boys—Bradley, Zachary, and Benjamin—continue to brighten my days more than I can ever tell them. My brother, Mike, and my father, Ron, offered healthy perspectives and sympathetic ears. When I was an undergraduate, my mother, Ruth, would remind me that my "main job was to study"; when I became an assistant professor and mother of three, she helped me to find a tenuous balance between those studies and my family. Even now, as I write these words, she is playing Parcheesi with a grandson. I hope she knows how deeply grateful I am, every day. And finally, I offer my love and thanks to my husband, David. For over fifteen years, he has been my first reader, my best reader, and my best friend. He is smart, kind, creative, and generous. Many of the central concepts and turns of phrase in this book emerged during late-night conversations at our kitchen table. He has made this book a better book and me a better person.

This research was supported by a grant-in-aid from the National Council of Teachers of English and by a summer faculty fellowship at Marquette University. Earlier versions of portions of this book were previously published in "Why Is Being Interdisciplinary So Very Hard to Do? Thoughts on the Perils and Promise of Interdisciplinary Pedagogy," *College Composition and Communication* 60.3 (© 2009 National Council of Teachers of English [NCTE]; reprinted with permission); "A Discourse-based Theory of Interdisciplinary Connections," *JGE: The Journal of General Education* 54.3 (2005): 171–95 (© 2005, Penn State University Press); "Toward a Theory of Interdisciplinary Connections: A Classroom Study of Talk and Text," *Research in the Teaching of English* 41.4 (© 2007, NCTE; reprinted with permission); and "Negotiating Individual Religious Identity and Institutional Religious Culture," *Negotiating Religious Faith in the Composition Classroom*, ed. Elizabeth Vander Lei and Bonnie L. Kyburz, pp 155–66 (Portsmouth, NH: Boynton/Cook, © 2005).

AGENTS OF INTEGRATION

Introduction

> [M]ost students experience the curriculum not as a connected conversation but as a disconnected series of courses that convey wildly mixed messages. As students go from course to course and subject to subject, the comparisons that the mind needs to identify points of contrast and common ground between disciplines and subfields are effaced.
>
> —Gerald Graff, *Clueless in Academe*

> It strikes me that the implications of what we know about transfer are very significant, even radical, not only for the ways writing might be taught but for the writing curriculum as a whole and the way courses relate to or "talk to" one another. It is rare in college and universities that we explicitly teach the transfer of knowledge and skills from one course to another or from one discipline to another. The question is how to construct a writing curriculum so that such instruction in transfer is commonplace, indeed a major feature of the curriculum.
>
> —David Smit, *The End of Composition Studies*

THE FIELD OF RHETORIC and composition long ago rejected the myth of autonomous literacy, recognizing that what constitutes good writing is defined by the participants in a given discourse community (or, more recently, activity system). The field has, nonetheless, largely maintained its faith in the transfer of learning. Yet, some concerns about transfer of learning have always been with us; the tales of failed (or at least deeply problematic) transfer are legion. Over twenty years ago, McCarthy (1987) offered the dismaying portrait of

This rich data set illustrates the manifold ways in which students are regularly making connections that often remain invisible.

RESEARCH METHODOLOGY

Context of Study

The classroom study that informs this book was conducted in a team-taught multidisciplinary sequence known formally as Interdisciplinary Humanities Seminar. "Interdisc" (as it is known colloquially) is offered to first-year honors students at a Catholic university on the East Coast and lasts three semesters. Each year, approximately twenty students are invited to fulfill many of the university's general education requirements by participating in the seminar. Participation in the Interdisc I–III sequence requires a significant commitment from both students and teachers. Students selected to participate in Interdisc are generally expected to complete the full three-semester sequence of courses. Throughout the sequence, the cohort of students remains constant, but each new semester brings a new combination of disciplines and professors.

I conducted my research during the second semester of the three-semester sequence. Interdisc II was composed of three distinct three-credit classes—literature, history, and religious studies—for which all eighteen students in the course enrolled.

The entire Interdisc sequence traces a chronology of Western civilizations from ancient Greece to twentieth-century Europe. The course I studied, Interdisc II, focuses specifically on medieval-, early-modern-, and Enlightenment-era Western civilizations.

As table 0.1 illustrates, each class period had a disciplinary designation, but professors attended and participated in each other's classes on a regular basis. Sessions with only one professor present were the exception. Because the sessions met back-to-back in the same room with all the same participants, discussions would sometimes go overtime or segue from one to the next without break. Generally, though, students kept separate notebooks for each component discipline and spoke of a given class period as belonging to a professor. As table 0.2 shows, each professor developed and graded his or her own assignments. Only one assignment—a collaborative, oral final exam—required students to integrate material from the various disciplines and was evaluated by all three professors.

Table 0.1

A typical week in Interdisciplinary Humanities Seminar II

Monday	Tuesday	Wednesday	Thursday
10–10:50	9:30–10:45	10–10:50	9:30–10:45
History: Chapter 6 *Middle Ages*	Literature: *Wife of Bath* (cont.)	History: excerpts Aquinas's *Treatise on Law*	Religious Studies: Aquinas's *Summa* (cont.)
11–11:50	11–12:15	11–11:50	11–12:15
Literature: *Wife of Bath's Prologue & Tale*	Religious Studies: Aquinas's *Summa*	Literature: *The Courtier*	History: Chapter 7 *Middle Ages*

Table 0.2

Interdisciplinary Humanities II assignments: The semester at a glance

	Interdisc Literature II	Interdisc History II	Interdisc Religious Studies II
Instructor	Professor Olivia S.	Professor Roger B.	Professor Thomas H.
Assignment 1	2–3 pp. on Chaucer	medieval diary	8–10 pp. on Aquinas
Assignment 2	3–4 pp. on *Faustus*	2 informal response papers	8–10 pp. comparative
Assignment 3	4–5 pp. open topic	French Revolution term paper	—
	Take-home midterm	Take-home midterm	Take-home midterm
	Take-home final	Take-home final	Take-home final

NOTE: The semester culminated in an oral final, taken in groups of three students, including presentation of a thesis that integrated information and insights from all three disciplines.

Certainly, this classroom is not typical of most undergraduate classrooms. The curricula were linked during planning sessions before the semester began. The professors attended each other's classes on a regular basis—listening, asking questions, pointing out connections. A small cohort of honors students took all three semesters of Interdisc together. And because Interdisc links three humanities courses, it is not necessarily typical of interdisciplinary courses, which can link STEM and social science disciplines as well as FYC courses.

Nevertheless, this class provides an appropriate basis for developing a theory of transfer. Because students received separate assignments and separate grades, the students experienced the three disciplinary strands of Interdisc as distinct. Interdisc is different in degree, not kind, from the traditional unconnected curriculum. The types of connections that students make between, say, a philosophy and a biology course might differ from the connections students forged in Interdisc: such a course might demand what Kelly (1996) calls "wide" interdisciplinarity, whereas the three humanities courses require "narrow" interdisciplinarity. However, I offer in this book a theory of how transfer operates—not a definitive claim. Future research in other contexts will determine the ways in which this theoretical framework adequately describes—or does not—the experiences of students and instructors more broadly.

Participants

Participating in this study were the eighteen students enrolled in Interdisc II (ten of whom agreed to be focal students) and their three instructors. All students—except one sophomore transfer—were first-year students in their second semester in the College of Liberal Arts and Sciences.

This was the second time this particular combination of teachers taught Interdisc II together. The history professor, Roger, had been teaching in the Interdisc program for over twenty years. (The Interdisc students addressed professors by their first names, so I will, too. All student and professor names are pseudonyms.) Roger had been teaching Interdisc with Thomas, the religious studies professor, for eight years. The newest member of this teaching team was the literature professor, Olivia; this was her second year of teaching Interdisc with Roger and Thomas and her third year at the university.

Data Collection

Throughout the semester, I collected a wide range of data.

- ✓ I attended and audiotaped every class session and took field notes.
- ✓ I used a written survey to collect demographic data and personal information.
- ✓ I collected all student papers (complete with professor comments) and drafts of papers (with peer-review comments) when available.
- ✓ I conducted a series of interviews with the ten focal students, consisting of three longer interviews (thirty to ninety minutes) at the beginning, middle, and end of the semester.
- ✓ I also conducted a series of shorter interviews (ten to thirty minutes) with focal students before and after they worked on papers for two of their three classes.
- ✓ I conducted two, forty-five- to ninety-minute interviews with each of the three professors.
- ✓ I videotaped six class periods and used those tapes to conduct three focus group interviews: two with focal students, a third with the professors.
- ✓ I photocopied the course notebooks of nine students (some were focal students, others were not) at the end of the semester.

Data Analysis

My analyses proceeded in several overlapping and iterative stages. During the first stage, I transcribed twenty-five class sessions selected with an effort to represent all three professors evenly throughout the semester. I coded each transcript, adapting methods of grounded theory (Strauss 1987). After several iterations of coding and memoing, I identified a taxonomy of interdisciplinary connections made in this particular classroom and used this taxonomy to analyze the relationship between interdisciplinary connections made in classroom discussion and student texts (see Nowacek 2007). As I conducted and expanded these analyses, I continued to read current work in genre theory and cultural historical activity theory. The iterative experience of reading such theory and working with my own empirical data set led me to further theorize the particular experience of interdisciplinarity (Nowacek 2005a) and the phenomenon of transfer more broadly. The earlier stages of analysis made it possible to identify the four avenues of transfer I identify in chapter 1; my readings in genre and activity theory also helped me to reconceptualize the role of genre in transfer. Using this revised taxonomy, I extended some earlier analyses of trends in student writing and conducted new analyses.

OVERVIEW

In chapter 1, I develop a theoretical framework for the underlying premise of this book: that transfer is best understood as an act of recontextualization. To develop the five principles of this framework, I draw on previous work in cognitive psychology, activity theory, and rhetorical genre theory, as well as my own analyses of student work.

In chapter 2, I build upon the five principles of transfer as recontextualization in order to develop the concept of *agents of integration*—a concept that foregrounds the rhetorical dimensions of transfer. This chapter turns to empirical study of the phenomenon of transfer and takes up two questions. How do institutional structures affect student and instructor perceptions of transfer? And what are the capacities that students develop in order to become agents of integration? Understanding students as agents of integration situates students' experiences as individual meaning-makers within an institutional context that often works against the recognition and valuing of transfer.

Chapter 3 focuses on the experience of instructors teaching for transfer. Instructors shift among a trio of roles: they are, as I argue in chapter 2, the *audience* for students working as agents to see and sell connections; they are also *agents* in their own right and on occasion *handlers* working to support the efforts of students-as-agents.

To better understand the challenges of teaching for transfer, I explore the work of the Interdisc instructors in each of these capacities; in particular, I examine the ways in which genres—with their constellations of associated knowledge domains, ways of knowing, identities, and goals—play an integral role in the phenomenon of transfer for teachers as well as students. The central question of the chapter is this: what are the exigencies and constraints that spoken and written classroom genres provide instructors teaching for transfer?

In chapter 4, I focus specifically on the transfer of writing-related knowledge across disciplinary contexts. Building on previous chapters that clarify the central role genre plays for agents of integration engaged in acts of transfer, I ask three distinct but ultimately related questions: What do students seem to know about genres? How do students make use of known genres when acquiring new genres? What can be learned about transfer of writing-related knowledge by examining a context not bound by the institutional limitations of first-year composition?

The final chapter explores the pedagogical implications of viewing students as agents of integration. In separate sections, I address the implications for first-year composition programs, writing centers, and future research. In light of the more robust understanding of transfer developed in the previous chapters, this final chapter offers a renewed hope for teaching for transfer across the curriculum.

1

Transfer as Recontextualization

STUDENTS TRANSFER KNOWLEDGE across disciplinary boundaries more often than current theories of transfer expect or acknowledge. There are significant obstacles to transfer, certainly. Many students do not make connections when they ought or make them visible when they might—true. Nevertheless, spending a semester with ten undergraduate students—sitting in on their courses, interviewing them about their papers, joining them for the occasional lunch—convinced me that students' efforts to connect knowledge across boundaries are not always recognized or valued, either by their instructors or by the theories that seek to explain these students' efforts.

If theories are bound by the data on which they are based, then it is no surprise that theories grown out of experimental labs and longitudinal studies do not account for the rich, diverse, and sometimes fugitive instances of transfer I observed over my fifteen weeks with these students. A richer, more accurate understanding of transfer requires a different theoretical framework.

This fact is not merely a point of curiosity for researchers. It influences classroom practice on the macro and micro levels. The facts are these: although relatively few research-based studies argue against the existence of transfer, very little classroom-based research illuminates the existence of transfer. In the absence of an empirically grounded theoretical framework, an abiding skepticism about students' abilities to connect what they've learned in one context to what they do in another has taken root. This skepticism takes the anecdotal form of faculty laments. It takes the institutional form of efforts like the Common Core State Standards Initiative, which narrows the complex act of writing to a set of discrete skills. It takes the form of increasingly common calls, like those of the Spellings Commission on the Future of Higher Education, to increase accountability in postsecondary education through assessment. Any assessment effort that attempts to measure the "value added" of a college education—an education comprising a polyphony of experiences, inside and outside the classroom—begins with the tacit assumption that students can and should transfer knowledge gained in one context, using it and building upon it in other contexts. But what if current theories of transfer inhibit the ability to recognize instances of transfer and obscure the institutional obstacles to making transfer visible? The inability to recognize students' acts of transfer has far-reaching (if not always immediately evident) consequences in individual classrooms and beyond.

This book develops the concept of agents of integration—a metaphor that foregrounds the various ways in which a successful act of transfer is a complex rhetorical act. To better understand the conditions that foster successful integration requires a richer understanding of the broader phenomenon of transfer. The current chapter articulates a theoretical foundation for understanding transfer—understanding transfer as recontextualization—that emerges from my own classroom-based research as well as prior theory and research. First I review the scholarship on transfer in the fields of psychology and of composition and rhetoric, pointing out the limitations of these prior theories, which do little to explain how individuals recognize the opportunity to draw connections. Then I introduce the idea of transfer as recontextualization—an idea developed through five principles.

THE QUESTION OF TRANSFER

Arguments against Transfer

Is transfer even possible? The answer in the scholarly literature, by and large, has been yes. But this orthodoxy has not gone unchallenged. In the appropriately titled *Transfer on Trial*, Douglas K. Detterman (1993) veers between definitions of transfer that are impossibly ambitious and meaninglessly vague. "Significant transfer," he writes, requires a "novel insight" and is therefore as rare as "volcanic eruptions and large earthquakes" (2). Detterman offers another definition of transfer as "the degree to which a behavior will be repeated in a new situation"—a definition he acknowledges is practically meaningless since "[i]n a trivial sense, all repeated behavior must be transferred" (4).

According to Detterman, most experimental studies that claim to have identified instances of transfer have instead simply prodded the participants to make connections. For instance, Mary L. Gick and Keith J. Holyoak's (1980) oft-cited study of analogical thinking found that when participants were first told the story of a military campaign that succeeded by attacking a fortress from multiple directions, participants presented with an analogous medical problem of how best to irradiate a tumor struggled to generate a solution. But when prompted to use the first story to help solve the second, over 90 percent succeeded (Gick and Holyoak 1980, 342). Detterman objects to calling this analogical problem solving transfer: "When subjects are told that previous material may be useful in the solution of a new problem, it hardly seems reasonable to refer to the solution of the new problem as the result of transfer" (Detterman 1993, 11).

I disagree, for reasons that are central to the argument of this book. As individuals move from context to context, they receive cues, both explicit and implicit, that suggest knowledge associated with a prior context may prove useful in the new context. A significant portion of this book is devoted to unpacking how those cues for transfer manifest and how individuals make sense of them. Spoken and written genres are a central mechanism for providing (or sometimes disguising) such cues.

Another variation of the transfer-is-impossible argument has appeared within the field of rhetoric and composition, as some scholars have argued for the abolition of first-year composition courses. These critics claim that a sociocultural theoretical framework offers no reason to expect transfer of writing abilities from FYC to other contexts. To illustrate the problem with thinking of "good writing" as an autonomous and automatically transferable skill rather than one qualified by a community of practice, David R. Russell (1995; Russell and Yañez 2003) has offered a compelling analogy. Most first-year composition courses, he claims, are not unlike a hypothetical course in general ball playing. He invites readers to imagine a course that purports to teach students to successfully handle balls by giving them opportunities to learn about and to play games such as football, baseball, and soccer. By the end of fifteen weeks, students may indeed have become more skilled at these three sports. But, Russell asks, to what degree can practice in these three sports prepare individuals to play golf or basketball or ping-pong? Not much—for abilities that serve an individual well in one context (the ability to intercept a pass with one's hands in football or basketball) might prove useless in another context (playing golf) or even a hindrance in another (soccer).

The analogy is a powerful one, but Russell's argument is not that transfer is entirely impossible—only that "learning is not neatly 'transferred' from one activity to another" (Russell and Yañez 2003, 336). Ultimately, to the extent that scholars like Russell argue against transfer, it is to challenge limited understandings of transfer—not to argue against its existence. Instead, the scholarly literature on transfer has focused on the exact nature and mechanisms of transfer.

General versus Local Knowledge

Scholarly preoccupation with transfer of knowledge across disciplinary domains can be traced back at least to the fourth century B.C.E.: in his *Rhetoric*, Aristotle (1991) argues for the value of both the *koina topoi* (which are "not concerned with any underlying subject" [46]) and the *idia topoi* (which are "particular and specific" [47]). Transfer research in cognitive psychology enacts a similar debate over the relative importance of general cognitive strategies and local contextual knowledge.

Formal discipline theory, for instance, suggested that schoolboys should study subjects like Latin because cognitive abilities are like muscles: they can be exercised and made stronger and used in any context (a view later discredited by E. L. Thorndike). Arguments that explain transfer as a function of general rather than local knowledge then took another persistent guise: an emphasis on cognitive abilities that, if learned at a sufficient level of abstraction, might be applied in any situation. M. T. H. Chi and colleagues (1981, 1982) argue that expert problem solvers in physics are able to look beyond surface-level similarities (like inclined planes) to see the more abstract and fundamental features of the problem to be solved (like conservation of energy). Similarly, George Polya (1957) presents an approach to mathematical problem solving that emphasizes general heuristics: "Generality is an important characteristic of the questions and suggestions contained in our list. . . . Their use is not restricted to any subject-matter" (2). Such studies assume different time frames and learning curves for the acquisition of expert knowledge but share a belief that general cognitive strategies and abstract mental schema are widely transferable.

But this conclusion was dealt a severe blow by the research of William G. Chase and Herbert A. Simon (1973), who showed a chess-board, midgame, to three categories of participants: chess masters, skilled chess players, and chess novices. After allowing players to look at the board for five seconds, they asked the participants to re-create the positions of the pieces on the board. Not surprisingly, the chess masters could correctly place many more pieces than the merely skilled and novice players (sixteen pieces, rather than eight or four pieces). However, when the researchers conducted the same experiment with pieces placed in positions that would not be meaningful within an actual game, the extraordinary performance of the chess masters vanished: all participants placed only two or three pieces correctly. In other words, experts possess not a general cognitive ability (like the ability to memorize a board quickly) but instead call on a rich repertoire of local knowledge (positions and moves that are meaningful within a chess game) to help chunk and remember what they see.

Theoretically, the general/local debate has generated an informative scholarly literature. Pedagogically, however, the extremes of this debate leave instructors wondering how they might teach for transfer. David N. Perkins and Gavriel Salomon (1988, 1989) argue that the problem with the debate over the relative value of general and contextualized skills—even within those approaches that advocate a synthesis—is that they begin by assuming that general and local knowledge are in fact separable. "The heart of the synthesis we would like to suggest," write Perkins and Salomon, "challenges this dichotomy. There are general cognitive skills; but they always function in contextualized ways" (1989, 19). To challenge the general/local dichotomy, Perkins and Salmon offer the concepts of low-road and high-road transfer.

Low-road transfer is a largely unconscious mechanism, possible only when an individual has a rich understanding of the subject that has become automatic; most often, low-road transfer takes place between two very similar contexts. Consider the example of learning to drive a car and then getting behind the wheel of a small truck: "The new context almost automatically activates the patterns of behavior that suit the old one: the steering wheel begs one to steer it, the windshield invites one to look through it, and so on." High-road transfer, in contrast, connects very dissimilar contexts and requires "deliberate mindful abstraction of skill or knowledge from one context for application in another" (Perkins and Salomon 1988, 25).

The problem of transfer is not inexorable but is instead what Perkins and Salomon call the Bo Peep problem of transfer: too often, teachers assume that transfer will simply happen, in the way that if left alone Bo Peep's sheep will come home. We cannot, Perkins and Salomon argue, assume it will happen on its own. Instead, we must teach for transfer. In situations where transfer is possible but does not occur, the problem is "inert" knowledge (Perkins and Salomon 1988, 23). Particularly helpful is this theory's emphasis on transfer as the act of an individual mind. Transfer will happen only when an individual recognizes similar elements: sometimes that happens because the "perceptual similarit[ies]" are immediately evident to an individual, other times transfer requires "deliberate . . . connection making" (Perkins and Salomon 1988, 27). Less robust are the pedagogical implications Perkins and Salomon draw from the high-road–low-road distinction.

To instructors wishing to teach for transfer, Perkins and Salomon offer two primary strategies: bridging (meant to promote high-road transfer) and hugging (meant to promote low-road transfer). Yet, despite the promise that such approaches "write a relatively simple recipe for teaching for transfer" and "practically guarante[e]" successful transfer, the challenge of transfer remains a sticky one for writing instructors (1988, 30).

Teaching for Transfer in the Writing Classroom

Recent transfer scholarship in rhetoric and composition has adopted a wide range of methodological approaches: longitudinal studies focusing on student self-reports and writing (Beaufort 1999, 2007; Carroll 2002; Wardle 2007), surveys and focus groups plumbing faculty perceptions (Nelms and Dively 2007), focus groups gathering student perceptions (Bergmann and Zepernick 2007), theory building that rests on synthesis of theory from other fields and reanalysis of previous empirical studies (Smit 2004).

Throughout this scholarship, there is general agreement that transfer can and does happen: students report transfer of "the basics," including writing strategies related to "research, style, audience, organization, and analysis" (Carroll 2002, 74), and instructors report seeing capabilities developed in first-year composition courses in subsequent classes (Nelms and Dively 2007). Yet, there is further agreement that transfer is difficult to predict or control.

Several hypotheses about what impedes transfer have emerged. If writing abilities developed in first-year composition courses are not used in subsequent classes, it may be because students see no need for them—either because the assignments are simple enough to succeed without the strategies or because students avoid more challenging assignments (Wardle 2007, 74). Or it may be because students conceptualize first-year English as "subjective" and "creative" writing and therefore irrelevant to their work in disciplinary contexts (Bergmann and Zepernick 2007, 130–32). The teachers whom Nelms and Dively interviewed hypothesized that students may not transfer writing knowledge from first-year composition to subsequent classes because of a basic inclination to compartmentalize (223); if such an inclination exists, it can only be exacerbated by a lack of shared vocabulary that might help students make connections among disparate contexts (227).

Currently, most reported instances of transfer seem to be low-road transfer—connections made tacitly, between relatively similar situations, by students drawing on knowledge that they have developed over time. The answer to the question of how to support high-road transfer seems to rest primarily on helping students to see a need for transfer. Without a perceived need, transfer in new and dissimilar contexts will not happen (Wardle 2007; Smit 2004, 124, 130). Anne Beaufort (2007) quotes Perkins and Salomon on ways to bridge and hug (150), Lee Ann Carroll encourages instructors to "share their own 'tips of the trade'" and "'remind' students to use strategies they have previously learned" (75), and Elizabeth Wardle (2007) suggests that "meta-awareness about writing, language, and rhetorical strategies in FYC may be the most important ability our course can cultivate" (82).

These are valuable contributions to our understanding of transfer, but the question of how exactly individuals recognize similarities and differences between contexts, either consciously or tacitly, remains unanswered. We lack a theory of transfer that would allow us to be more specific about how hugging and bridging work, about what meta-awareness recognizes. In short, the nature of these metacognitive abilities needs to be further qualified and described. To put our faith in unspecified metacognitive abilities is tantamount to pointing to a black box in which a general cognitive ability magically operates.

The fundamental constraints and exigencies for transfer come not from the black box of metacognitive knowledge but from, among other sources, genres that shape and are shaped by the social and rhetorical interactions of individuals. The discursive space that individuals negotiate—that they are situated amidst and seek to make connections within—is fundamentally a "genred discursive space" (Bawarshi 2003, 14; Bazerman 2002, 17). Metacognitive awareness may assist in the process of transfer but is not *necessary* for transfer.

It is spoken and written genres that provide both the shape and the means of reshaping the discursive spaces within which acts of transfer occur. Genre is not the only cue for transfer, but it is a powerful and underappreciated cue. By recognizing the power of genres—and helping students to do the same—instructors can help facilitate mindful transfer. This claim echoes arguments advanced by Anis Bawarshi (2003), Beaufort (1999, 2007), and most especially Amy Devitt (2004). But there has not yet been a systematic analysis of how antecedent genres make up the genred discursive space in which individuals perceive the need and opportunity for transfer.

Much as Chase and Simon found that the memory of chess pieces was cued by knowledge of routinized chess placements and moves, I argue that the recognition of unexpected similarities and connections can be cued by the routinized epistemic spaces genres provide. The remainder of this chapter and this book offers a theoretical framework for transfer that specifies what transfer looks like for students and instructors and interrogates how spoken and written genres offer exigencies and constraints for students trying to make connections and teachers trying to facilitate connections.

TRANSFER AS RECONTEXTUALIZATION: A GENRE-MEDIATED CONCEPTION

Previous scholarship takes too limited a view of transfer. Transfer is both more common and more complex than research currently recognizes. Unwilling to relinquish the term *transfer*, I wish instead to enlarge its meaning by speaking of "transfer as recontextualization." These two terms—*transfer* and *recontextualization*—are largely interchangeable, but by using the term *recontextualization*, I mean to invoke the specific conception of transfer elaborated in the five principles that constitute this chapter.

Central to this concept of transfer as recontextualization is the role of genre. Genre as conceived in recent rhetorical theory diverges significantly from traditional literary understandings of genre as the formal properties of various types of writing. Recent genre theory conceptualizes genre not as a literary category but as a rhetorical act. To say that genre is a rhetorical act means, among other things, that genre not only provides a sociocognitive resource for crafting a response to a social situation but it also provides a resource for interpreting (and indeed constructing) that situation in the first place.

This view of genre builds on the work of Mikhail M. Bakhtin (1981, 1986), who argued that genre provides a way of understanding how utterances can be stable and often predictable but not predetermined over time. Utterances are inextricably linked to their social context, and every social context (e.g., passing a colleague in the hallway, going to the public library) includes repeated social interactions or tasks to be accomplished (e.g., exchange of pleasantries, issuance of a library card). Bakhtin explains that over time "a particular function (scientific, technical, commentarial, business, everyday) and the particular conditions of speech communication specific for each sphere give rise to particular genres, that is, certain relatively stable thematic, compositional, and stylistic types of utterances" (1986, 64).

These relatively stable types of utterances, or genres, ease communication: we can toss off the predictable "Hello, how are you?" / "Fine, you?" exchange without breaking stride; we fill out preprinted forms to get a library card. Without them, we would reinvent the communicative wheel with each interaction. Genres help us predict the responses of others without predetermining them. Rarely do our colleagues reply as we rush past each other, "Not well at all; my mother is ill, and I'm feeling depressed"—but when they do, it cues us that we have now entered into a very different type of social interaction. Genres also help us understand our own obligations: we know we must come to the library with a form of written identification rather than a friend to vouch for our name and address.

Genres are thus a social and rhetorical resource that helps individuals both to generate (by choosing to talk about family illness rather than say, "I'm fine," we create a very different social and rhetorical situation) and to interpret (when the unexpected response comes, we realize "Ahh—we're not doing hallway pleasantries; my friend needs help"). In Carolyn Miller's (1984) oft-quoted phrasing, genres are "typified rhetorical actions based in recurrent situations" (159). As such, genres are not merely a set of textual conventions but encompass an entire constellation of associated social relations, goals, identities, ways of knowing, and even knowledge domains. Throughout this book, I refer to this constellation of associations as the genred discursive space within which individuals operate and make meaning. Recognizing the existence of this constellation of genre associations, associations that can be either tacit or explicit, is central to understanding the relationship between genre and the phenomenon of transfer.

There is an important parallel between theories of transfer and theories of genre. Theories of transfer assume that an individual is moving among fundamentally *different* situations and seeking to identify some similarity. Dale H. Schunk (2004) defines transfer as "knowledge being applied in *new* ways, in *new* situations, or in old locations with *different* content" (217; emphasis added); Detterman (1993) defines transfer as "the degree to which a behavior will be repeated in a *new* situation" (4; emphasis added). Metaphors of application, bridging, hugging, generalizing, and crossing boundaries abound.

Conversely, theories of genre assume that individuals find themselves in fundamentally *similar* situations and draw on socially constructed and constitutive genres in order to minimize the sense of difference in these different situations. Bakhtin (1986) defines speech genres as "*relatively stable* thematic, compositional, and stylistic types of utterances" (64); Miller (1984) defines genres as "*typified* rhetorical actions based in *recurrent* situations" (159); Catherine F. Schryer (1994) identifies genre as a "*stabilized-for-now or stabilized-enough* site of social and ideological action" (108) (emphasis added to all quotes). In all these conceptualizations, genre, though dynamic, is a way to avoid reinventing the wheel, a way of seeing general trends.

And yet, genre, a way of dealing with recurrent social and intellectual contexts, is a powerful way of understanding transfer, commonly understood as the negotiation of very different social and intellectual contexts. The key to this seeming paradox is that genres serve as "the guideposts we use to explore the unfamiliar" (Bazerman 1997, 19). Because they serve as the nexus between stability and change, genres are powerfully positioned as a means of identifying and responding to a sense that there is a need that must be met or an opportunity that can be realized by making connections between various contexts. A genre's constellation of associations provides ready avenues of connection.

Five principles further unpack this idea of transfer as an act of recontextualization.

Principle 1

Transfer understood as recontextualization recognizes multiple avenues of connection among contexts, including knowledge, ways of knowing, identities, and goals.

Based on my analyses of classroom talk and student writing, I have identified four avenues of connection, four resources that individuals employ as they draw connections among various contexts: knowledge, ways of knowing, identity, and goals.

This conceptualization of the ways in which individuals forge connections among previously distinct contexts is strongly informed by activity theory. As articulated by Yrjo Engeström (1987) and developed in its North American applications (Dias 2000; Russell 1995, 1997), activity theory proves especially useful for understanding transfer as recontextualization because it draws attention to the transit of people and ideas among varied and often competing activity systems. Although the traditional view of discourse communities acknowledged that people could participate in multiple discourse communities, it did little to help conceptualize the complexity that results when multiple communities overlap—either because of the participation of an individual in multiple discourse communities or because of larger social changes that bring discourse communities into sustained contact. Activity theory, in contrast, provides a vocabulary and a unit of analysis that highlight the connections that result when multiple activity systems intersect.

An activity system, in its most basic representation (see fig. 1.1), consists of four elements: subjects, either an individual or a collection of people; an object of attention and the intended outcome (official or unofficial) that drives activity in the system; and the mediational (cultural and discursive as well as physical) tools used within the system.

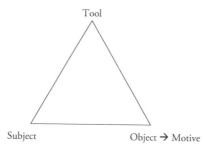

Figure 1.1. Basic elements of an activity system. Adapted from Engeström's *Learning by Expanding*

The world of human action, in this view, is replete with such activity systems; individuals participate, often simultaneously, in multiple activity systems. A mediational tool used in one activity system (for instance, the review essay assigned in an undergraduate history class) can be used in other systems (such as the field of professional journalism or the academic discipline of history) in order to achieve very different motives (Russell and Yáñez 2003). Activity theory helps us to see that borrowed materials are never devoid of resonances from other activity systems; individuals using mediational tools from one disciplinary activity system within another face a series of complex and often unconscious negotiations.

These four avenues of recontextualization can be mapped with some success onto the terms of the activity-system triangle: knowledge (what activity theory identifies as the object of an activity system), ways of knowing (the mediational tools in an activity system), identity (the subjects of an activity system), and goals (the overriding intended outcome or motive of an activity system).

Why not simply use the language of activity theory? Frankly, some readers find it inaccessible. More importantly, although the four avenues of connection line up relatively neatly with activity theory, they are not entirely synonymous with the terms of the activity-theory triangle. Most notably, ways of knowing (which are the intellectual activities that individuals engage in) cannot be equated with mediational tools (which are the resources subjects might use to engage in ways of knowing). This imperfect mapping might be further complicated by comparing the four avenues to Engeström's full activity-systems model, which includes rules, community, and division of labor. In short, the four avenues are not predetermined by my reading of activity theory. This taxonomy is grounded in my empirical work with classroom data—work motivated by a variety of research questions and theoretical frameworks—and has roots in an earlier investigation of interdisciplinary connections. The parallels to activity theory affirm rather than determine the value of this taxonomy.

In earlier research (Nowacek 2007), I read twenty-five transcripts of discussion in the Interdisc classroom, looking for instances of interdisciplinary connection. From that focus on interdisciplinary connections, I developed a tripartite schema of resources that individuals draw on to forge interdisciplinary connections: content, propositions, and ways of knowing. This earlier study convinced me that knowledge and ways of knowing are powerful resources for making connections among various disciplinary contexts.

In another study drawing from that same classroom data, I examined the influence of institutional religious culture on students' interpretations of task in their religious studies and literature classes (Nowacek 2005b). I found that students' understandings of the goal of an assignment were strongly influenced by their religious identities; furthermore, students' identities and personal goals were often defined in solidarity with or in opposition to what they perceived as the goals of the Catholic university they attended. This study convinced me that personal identities and the goals of an activity system have a powerful and complicated influence on the work students do as they move among activity systems. Together, my prior analyses and my readings in activity theory research helped me to identify the four major avenues of recontextualization when two contexts (or activity systems) collide.

When I speak of *knowledge*, I have in mind both content (the primary texts, historical figures and events, authors, and so on that are ostensibly the subject matter of a discipline or other activity system) and propositions (arguments frequently made by participants in a given activity system; propositions are thus reminiscent of Arthur N. Applebee, Robert Burroughs, and Anita Stevens's [2000] concept of ongoing curricular "conversation" rather than J. L. Austin's [1962] and J. R. Searle's [1969] use of the term). Every class period contained multiple propositions (e.g., John Milton's portrayal of Eve is protofeminist; the movie *The Mission* does not provide a historically accurate portrait of Catholic missionary work), and some propositions were argued throughout the semester (e.g., history is not teleological).

By *ways of knowing*, I mean the intellectual activities that individuals engage in to articulate and support propositions, such as the gathering and interpretation of evidence. This concept echoes

Charles Bazerman's (1988) focus on disciplinary epistemologies and Applebee, Burroughs, and Stevens's (2000) notion of "conventions" that reflect larger disciplinary conversations. Ways of knowing also encompass the rhetorical domain of knowledge that Cheryl Geisler (1994) and Russell and Yañez (2003) identify as key for meaningful general education studies.

By _identities_, I mean an individual's understanding of his or her role, capacities, affiliations, and worth in a given social context—as well as that individual's perceptions of other people's evaluations of his or her role, capacities, affiliations, and worth. This definition emerges from observations of students identifying themselves in various ways (as a feminist, a scientist, a "slacker") but also resonates with Neil Gross's (2008) work on "intellectual self-concept," which

> holds that intellectuals tell themselves and others stories about who they are qua intellectuals: about their distinctive interests, dispositions, values, capacities, and tastes. These stories . . . involve a thinker describing herself or himself as an intellectual of a particular type—and once they become established they may exert a powerful effect on her or his future thought, inclining the thinker to embrace certain ideas over against others. (263–64)

I am reminded of Henry, one of the students in my classroom research, who saw himself as a "math and science guy" struggling with literature papers. I'm also reminded of Betty, whose identity as a non-Catholic became central to her interpretation of task and invention strategies. As individuals make connections among various disciplinary and social contexts, the identities associated with each context prove a significant avenue of connection (a claim that resonates with the emphasis of Christine Pearson Casanave [2002] and others on the importance of identity in the development of genre knowledge).

Goals are not altogether separable from identities, but recognizing goals as a distinct avenue of connection highlights the complicated relationship between the desires of the individual and the motives of larger communities. Goals can operate as cause and as effect. In some cases, an individual's goals may be tightly bound up with his or her sense of identity, and he or she may embrace and defend them despite resistance from other individuals or institutions. In other cases, an individual's goals may be largely defined by a community with which he or she feels affiliated. On occasion, these goals (of the person and the larger community or of two communities to which a single individual belongs) may be in conflict. The act of recontextualizing goals can thus be a powerful but problematic act of transfer. Such transfer can invest activities and identities and knowledge with new meanings and resonance and purpose, but it can also work against any such productive synthesis.

Principle 2

Transfer understood as recontextualization recognizes that transfer is not only mere application; it is also an act of reconstruction.

One of the most persistent metaphors for transfer is the metaphor of application. Understanding transfer as application implies bringing knowledge or skills from an earlier context into contact with a later context, the earlier context shedding light on and changing the perception of the later. Transfer *is* often an act of application. Chapter 2 describes a student applying knowledge gained in his history class to a paper written for literature class: to support the claim that knowledge equals power, he provided the example of Martin Luther. This example did not inspire the student's reading of *Doctor Faustus*, but it did serve as an example to support a claim.

However, transfer is not always a simple matter of application. When transfer is experienced not as application but as an act of reconstruction, both the old and new contexts—as well as what is being transferred—may be understood differently as a result. One context may provide a way of seeing possibilities where none existed before: working to define a topic for her term paper on the French Revolution, another student drew on her identity as well as her knowledge, ways of knowing, and goals as a feminist to see an entire field of possibilities.

Transfer as reconstruction might be helpfully understood as similar to what Veronica Boix-Mansilla (2005) describes as "interdisciplinary understanding"—something she defines as "the capacity to integrate knowledge and modes of thinking drawn from two or more disciplines to produce a cognitive advancement . . . in ways that would have been unlikely through single disciplinary means" (16). The first student's knowledge of Luther, although useful, provided no such "cognitive advancement"; it provided a brick in the building that was his paper on *Doctor Faustus*—an example of transfer as application. The second student's identity as a feminist, however, provided not just a brick but an entirely new blueprint—an example of transfer as reconstruction.

Both application and reconstruction exemplify the phenomenon of transfer, but their significant differences make it important to name and distinguish them. The term *recontextualization* is an umbrella term meant to encompass both types of transfer: the simpler act of application and the more complex act of reconstruction.

Principle 3
Transfer understood as recontextualization recognizes that transfer can be both positive and negative and that there is a powerful affective dimension of transfer.

Imagine a child who plays baseball. Through practice and coaching, a baseball player learns to hold the bat, to fix his or her stance as the pitch comes toward home plate, and to swing, drop the bat, and run. What happens when a child who has played a great deal of baseball is given a tennis racquet and a ball thrown toward him or her? Very likely that child will hold the racquet and swing with both hands—just like a bat.

Is this transfer of knowledge and skill useful, or is it an example of what is often termed *negative transfer*? The answer to that question depends on the standards of assessment: holding the racquet with two hands may indeed help our baseball player hit the tennis ball with considerable strength, but tennis players use several different grips. A two-handed backhand is an important capacity for many tennis players, but so is a one-handed grip that expands the player's ability to cover an entire court effectively. Holding the racquet with two hands, if it discourages the development of a one-handed grip, might be considered an instance of negative transfer.

But what if hitting the tennis ball with power inspires in our baseball player some real enthusiasm for playing tennis, providing enough satisfaction to continue with the sport? What if hitting the ball with power encourages the child to see him- or herself as an athlete, a self-definition that might significantly affect the continued process of transfer of knowledge and skill between the domains of baseball and tennis? Furthermore, what if the experience of having played baseball eventually enables the child to recognize at some level of consciousness the significant differences between hitting a baseball and hitting a tennis ball?

This analogy not only suggests the difficulty of assessing whether transfer is positive or negative (the answer to that question will depend on the assessment criteria) but also spotlights the affective dimension of transfer. Again and again, the students in this book described to me a real excitement and satisfaction that came with making connections. As we sat and talked, I could watch their eyes brighten, their brows furrow, their hands reach out as if to touch something nearly in their grasp. They spoke with pride and some-times frustration about these moments when things seemed to be coming together, when their studies started (even in maddeningly incomplete ways) to inform one another.

Transfer, in short, is not simply an intellectual accomplishment; for many students, it is an emotional experience: transfer as revela-tion, as the "a-ha!" moment. When students sense an opportunity to connect what they have been learning, they want to chase those connections—as a means of invention, yes, but also for personal satisfaction. As the case studies in chapter 2 illustrate, making these connections did not always result in stronger papers. Sometimes a lower grade might be attributed to an act of transfer. To adopt a view of transfer as recontextualization, then, is to recognize that evaluations of "positive" and "negative" transfer might be assessed not solely according to performance on an academic assignment but also within the individual student's conception of self and larger trajectory of intellectual and emotional development.

Principle 4

Transfer understood as recontextualization recognizes that written and spoken genres associated with these contexts provide an exigence for transfer.

How do individuals recognize or create the opportunity to forge an actual connection between, say, the knowledge of the Reformation they associate with their religious studies class and their reading of John Donne's poetry in a literature class? One answer lies in the social and rhetorical mechanisms of genre. Transfer is made possible by genres and more specifically by the genred discursive spaces that make up various activity systems. Genre is an exigence for transfer.

Previous scholarship has recognized a role for genre in transfer. Beaufort (2007) identifies genre knowledge as one of five knowledge domains drawn on by expert writers able to transfer their writing abilities from context to context (19). Mary Jo Reiff and Anis Bawarshi (forthcoming) have begun to theorize the relationship between a student's ability to transfer genre knowledge across boundaries and the use of what they call "'not' talk." Devitt (2004) argues that a FYC curriculum focused on genre awareness and carefully chosen antecedent genres might facilitate transfer. However, to say that genre is an exigence for transfer means something quite different.

Within genre studies, *exigence* is generally understood as the recurring social situation that calls forth a stabilized-for-now genre. This turn of phrase—"genre is the exigence for transfer"—recasts exigence as an individual's felt need to draw a connection. The exigence for transfer is the genred discursive space that helps individuals recognize and make a connection to something familiar in a new situation. Genres associated with one context—because they are experienced as a constellation of tacit and conscious associations—can cue an individual to make connections to knowledge domains, ways of knowing, identities, and goals associated with another, previously unrelated context. Genres are a place where the sense of exigence for transfer (either conscious or tacit) resides.

This claim presumes an intertextual view of genres. The concept of intertextuality, as developed by genre theorists, has focused on the interrelations of genres in the form of genre sets and repertoires and metagenres (see, for instance, Devitt's [2004] analysis of the interrelations of multiple genres used by tax accountants). The intertextual nature of genres makes transfer possible. The phenomenon of transfer, however, takes the individual as its unit of analysis. *Intertextuality* describes the interrelations of genres; *transfer* describes the individual act of cognition that recognizes those interrelations. An individual might recognize (however dimly) the potential for transfer because he or she recognizes some possibility of connecting the constellation of knowledge domains, ways of knowing, identities, and goals associated with one genre and context to another.

For example, asked by their history professor to compose a "medieval diary," many students wrote entries that perfectly satisfied their instructor's expectations: they focused on the material details of life on a medieval manor. Other students wrote texts focused on the psychological concerns of their subjects; these more personal approaches seemed to be invited by the identities and goals associated with the genre of "diary." The identities and goals associated with the genre of diary encouraged students to reconstruct the assignment in light of their other literary readings and religious preoccupations, readings and preoccupations easily associated with the goals and identities of the diary.

Genre can also, by virtue of these same associations, obscure possible connections between contexts. Chapter 3 recounts the example of two instructors breaking their usual patterns of relatively limited interaction. The instructors identified this exchange as a moment of positive interdisciplinary interaction. The students, however, expressed frustration bordering on anger about this same moment. Why? Because the instructors were breaking out of their usual patterns of interaction, out of their usual identities and roles. The shift was difficult and, in the students' eyes, inappropriate. Genred discursive spaces can thus confound instructors' efforts to teach for transfer.

In my formulation, genre remains a typified response to the exigence of a recurring social situation. Exigence is still a situation that calls forth genre. But genre itself also serves as an exigence, making visible (in ways that are both conscious and unconscious) possibilities for connections. The experience of occupying a particular genred discursive space—with its attendant identities and goals, its associated knowledge domains and ways of knowing—can suggest to individuals the possibility of connecting two previously distinct contexts. Genre is not the only exigence for transfer, but it is a powerful one that has been underappreciated even in the genre studies scholarship.

Principle 5

Transfer understood as recontextualization recognizes that meta-awareness is an important, but not a necessary, element of transfer.

Increasingly in rhetoric and composition, meta-awareness has been seen as the lynchpin of transfer, the sine qua non. Wardle (2007), for example, has concluded that meta-awareness may be one of the most valuable and portable skills students develop in first-year composition. This emphasis on the role of metacognition in transfer resonates with work on the role of reflection in writing instruction. Kathleen Blake Yancey (1992, 1996), for instance, has convincingly argued that without reflection, the writing portfolio is simply a folder of work; frequent and integrated reflection is a powerful way to facilitate metacognition, allowing students to critically engage with their prior work and knowledge within a new context.

I do not dispute the value of metacognitive awareness in facilitating transfer. However, the process of making connections exists on a spectrum. On one end of the spectrum are instances of transfer that happen relatively easily and are a tacit, unconscious process: low-road transfer. On the other end of the spectrum are those occasions when the process of connecting knowledge, ways of knowing, identities, or goals from one activity system to another is a difficult endeavor, requiring explicit attention and effort: high-road transfer.

To better understand the role of meta-awareness in transfer as recontextualization, Bakhtin's notions of heteroglossia and dialogization prove especially useful. To describe language as heteroglossic is, according to Bakhtin (1981), to recognize that language is stratified within our consciousness, that we use different languages for different purposes. To describe language as dialogized is to make a more specific claim about the commingling of those various languages in an individual's consciousness. To illustrate the differences between heteroglossic and dialogized consciousness, Bakhtin offers the example of a heteroglossic peasant with nondialogized consciousness who "prayed to God in one language, sang songs in another, spoke to his family in a third, and, when he began to dictate petitions to the local authorities through a scribe, he tried speaking yet a fourth language" (295–96). Different as they were, these languages

> were not dialogically coordinated in the linguistic consciousness of the peasant; he passed from one to the other without thinking, automatically: each was indisputably in its own place, and the place of each was indisputable. He was not yet able to regard one language . . . through the eyes of another language. (296)

The languages of various disciplinary activity systems often coexist in a similar way. The university is an undeniably heteroglot place where stratifications of language abound. For many individuals, these disciplinary languages remain heteroglossic, and the differences among them are not consciously recognized, much less dialogized. The results of dialogization, however, can be profound:

> As soon as a critical interanimation of languages began to occur in the consciousness of our peasant . . . the inviolability and predetermined quality of these languages came to an end, and the necessity of actively choosing one's orientation among them began. (1981, 296)

One important implication of understanding transfer as an act of recontextualization involves this process of dialogization. Such an understanding also resonates with Engeström's (1987) idea of "learning by expanding."

When activity systems overlap, either because an individual is moving among systems or because sociological changes have brought two previously distinct activity systems into sustained contact, the possibility for transfer exists. If there is no conflict between the two activity systems or if the knowledge, ways of knowing, identities, or goals are so well learned and integrated that one easily overrides the other, unconscious, low-road transfer may occur.

But if, for example, the goals of one activity system conflict with those of another, high-road transfer may occur—if there is to be transfer at all. In Bakhtinian terms, this is when dialogization may take place; the individual is forced to recognize the contradictions among the activity systems, must cease to see them as natural and inviolable, and must consciously orient him- or herself among them. Such a conflict is what Engeström and other activity theorists identify as "a psychological double bind." Double binds are those uncomfortable and perhaps inevitable situations in which individuals experience contradictions within or between activity systems but cannot articulate any meta-awareness of those contradictions. They are those scenarios in which an individual "receives two messages or commands which deny each other—and the individual is unable to comment on the messages" (Engeström 1987, chap. 3).

However, such double binds are a double-edged pedagogical sword. They can be baffling and even incapacitating for individuals, but when these conflicts push individuals to meta-awareness and individuals are able to "make a metacommunicative statement" about the conflict (Engeström 1987, chap. 3), double binds can also facilitate higher-order thinking and critical insight. Engeström describes such outcomes as "learning by expanding."

Given this view of activity systems and the relations among them, the phenomenon of transfer can be understood as occupying a spectrum (see table. 1.1), from a dim recognition of the coexistence of multiple but apparently independent activity systems to a mindful awareness of the overlap and interanimation of those activity systems.

This mapping of the spectrum highlights two important points. First, a lack of transfer, what Perkins and Salomon (1988) describe as the Bo Peep problem of inert knowledge, might be explained in at least two ways: it might be the result of an individual's heteroglossic failing to draw any connection at all between two distinct contexts. Or it might be the result of a double bind—one in which an individual has, at some level, recognized a conflict between two distinct contexts but cannot resolve (or perhaps even consciously recognize) the conflict.

Table 1.1.

Meta-awareness and transfer

	No transfer	Transfer	Integration
Perkins and Salomon	inert knowledge	low-road transfer	high-road transfer
Bakhtin	heteroglossia	dialogization	fully dialogized consciousness
Engeström	double bind	no significant conflict	learning by expanding

Second, the fully dialogized consciousness implied by Engeström's concept of learning by expanding and Perkins and Salomon's notion of high-road transfer is one important dimension of transfer—a dimension important enough to merit a distinguishing term. These notions not only suggest the importance of mindfulness and meta-awareness but also connote an act of transfer that has positive consequences for the student. I propose the term *integration* to designate acts of transfer on this end of the spectrum.

The phenomenon of transfer is widely varied (as the spectrum in table 1.1 suggests), but the term *integration* has been largely reserved to describe learning experiences that are intentional and successful. *Greater Expectations*, the influential Association of American Colleges and Universities (AAC&U) report on general education reform, provides (in the words of Andrea Leskes) a vision of students

> as "*integrative thinkers who can see connections* in seemingly disparate information and draw on a wide range of knowledge to make decisions." . . . This integrative capacity characterizes learners prepared for the twenty-first-century world: who are *intentional* about the process of acquiring learning, *empowered* by the mastery of intellectual and practical skills, *informed* by knowledge from various disciplines, and *responsible* for their actions and those of society. (Leskes 2005, iv; emphasis added)

Similarly, the AAC&U and Carnegie Foundation's joint "Statement on Integrative Learning" stresses the importance of intentionality on the part of both students and institutions (2004). In both cases, intentionality is acknowledged as central, and the positive outcomes of integration are never questioned. Although some acts of transfer may indeed be more fraught (for instance, double binds), the term *integrative learning* usually describes intentional and positive acts of connection-making. Consequently, throughout this book, when I refer to integration, I am referring to an act of transfer that assumes some degree of metacognitive awareness and a positive outcome for the student.

In summary, as the spectrum in table 1.1 illustrates, meta-awareness is an important element of "integration" and in some cases a necessary condition for transfer (more broadly defined) that enables successful recontextualization of elements that seem to be in conflict. But meta-awareness is not a necessary element of transfer in all cases, as transfer can and does sometimes happen unconsciously. This final principle is in keeping with the other four—particularly principle 4. Because genre serves as an exigence for transfer, the exigence can easily be experienced at a level of unconscious and unarticulated associations, rather than through a fully articulated meta-awareness.

CONCLUSION

This framework emerged from an iterative process of theoretical readings and working with empirical classroom-based research; it also provides the framework for analyzing that same data. The chapters that follow return to the five principles articulated in this chapter, using them to not only recognize a wider range of acts of transfer but also to better understand the circumstances that enable students to become agents of intentional and successful integration.

2

"I Finally Feel Like I've Really Learned Something": Students Becoming Agents of Integration

> You have to think about so much more than just literature when you're reading *Doctor Faustus*. I think I'm starting to do that more. . . . With the stuff that we're doing in history about the Reformation and humanism and how they all tie in with [*Doctor Faustus*]. And we're dealing with Donne now too, [asking] is this Protestant? We're talking about historical things and all that. I wouldn't have done that before; I would have just looked at the poem itself or *Doctor Faustus* itself.
>
> —Judy, an Interdisc student

> Reflection. Metacognition. Learning how to learn. Whatever the language or lineage, the idea of making students more self-aware and purposeful—more intentional—about their studies is a powerful one, and is key to fostering integrative learning. Assisting students to develop such capacities poses important challenges for campus reforms around teaching and learning.
> —Mary Huber and Pat Hutchings, *Integrative Learning* (2005)

THIS CHAPTER TURNS TO EMPIRICAL STUDY of the experience of students forging connections between various contexts—and in doing so develops the central metaphor of this book: *agents of integration*. This metaphor—insofar as it highlights the intersection between individual acts of cognition and the social contexts in which they occur—provides a compact and powerful way of understanding transfer as a rhetorical act, one that involves seeing and selling.

The concept of agents of integration—introduced here and extended in chapter 3 to teachers—provides a framework for understanding and a language for talking about the experiences of students in the classroom. It builds upon the basic framework of the five principles of transfer-as-recontextualization articulated in chapter 1. The concepts, language, and assumptions of those principles are woven through these case studies, providing their necessary foundation.

This chapter takes up two central questions. How do institutional structures affect student and instructor perceptions of transfer? And what are the capacities that students develop in order to become agents of integration? In the first epigraph, Judy suggests the importance of institutional structures: without the promptings of her instructors, she might not be making these interdisciplinary connections. But what exactly is the nature of the intentionality that Mary Taylor Huber and Pat Hutchings believe will help foster integrative learning? And how are perceptions of transfer related to institutional structures—for instructors as well as students?

The case studies that make up the heart of this chapter demonstrate that institutional structure has a significant effect on student and instructor perceptions of transfer. Because students' courses are disconnected from each other, because most instructors have few opportunities to learn what their colleagues are discussing and their students learning in other classes, the knowledge, ways of knowing, identities, and goals transferred from one class to another can seem meaningless.

This disconnection is a fact of life for most college and university instructors; the professors teaching Interdisc II were fortunate enough to have the institutional support to attend each other's classes. The challenges they still face in recognizing and responding to instances of student transfer throw into relief the challenges confronting instructors working within a traditional unconnected curriculum.

A common (and largely accurate) lament has been that the responsibility for integration has been unfairly shifted onto students; pedagogies and a curricular structure are needed to facilitate transfer (Bok 2006; Graff 2003; Huber et al. 2007). Indeed, these would help. However, my case studies argue against concluding that students are unable or unwilling to make many connections without highly developed curricular and pedagogical support. Such a view minimizes the central role instructors play in determining what gets valued as transfer.

THE TERMS OF TRANSFER

Current Understandings of "Negative" and "Zero" Transfer

Current theories generally presuppose that any instance of transfer will fall into one of three categories: positive, negative, or zero transfer. It is widely accepted that most students in most cases experience zero transfer, a scenario in which "one type of learning has no noticeable influence on subsequent learning" (Schunk 2004, 217). Negative transfer is most often understood as the inappropriate application of prior learning. Dale H. Schunk defines negative transfer as a scenario in which "prior learning interferes with subsequent learning or makes it more difficult" (217); M. L. Gick and K. J. Holyoak (1987) define it as a scenario in which initial training "produces a performance decrement" (10); applying these definitions to writing, Anne Beaufort (1999) describes negative transfer as instances in which the "norms of one discourse community were inappropriately transferred to a very different context for writing" (183). But these descriptors—"interfere," "decrement," "inappropriate"—normalize value judgments made about the usefulness and appropriateness of a given act of transfer.

The concept of negative transfer normalizes power relations. Current theories of transfer recognize that transfer is a cognitive act of an individual, but they have not sufficiently acknowledged that in the context of colleges and universities, the positive or negative nature of a given act of transfer is not evaluated solely by the student perceiving a connection. In a classroom, it is the instructor who has the power to decide whether to recognize and whether to reward or punish a given instance of transfer.

My case studies—because they are grounded in a thick, fifteen-week slice of students' lives—provide an unusual glimpse into the experiences of students. Although these case studies include instances of zero transfer, there are also many instances of students seeing and making connections. It is instructors who often do not, and for institutional reasons cannot, recognize those connections. There are, furthermore, occasions when instructors *do* see these acts of transfer but do not value them. There is an art to not simply seeing opportunities for integration but presenting the connection in a way that will seem appropriate to an instructor whose disciplinary work is now connecting with or being reconstructed by work in another discipline or within another nonacademic dimension of a student's life.

The concept of negative transfer also obscures the diversity of experiences lumped into this general category. The experience of a student whose prior knowledge of medieval religious figures (gained from reading *The Canterbury Tales* in literature class) interferes with her interpretation of an assignment for history would seem to qualify as negative transfer. But so, too, would a student's decision to recycle a paper written in high school when faced with a similar assignment in college. Negative transfer provides no vocabulary or theoretical insight for distinguishing these cases.

And what of a student who writes a successful paper for religious studies class but, relying on criteria developed in literature classes, describes it as a "cop-out"? There was interference—*and* there was academic success. Does the interference of prior learning constitute this experience as negative transfer? Or is the student's experience of interference outweighed by the instructor's positive appraisal? The term *negative transfer* renders invisible very different types of interference while normalizing power relations.

Agents of Integration

In response to these shortcomings, I offer the concept of agents of integration as a means of joining transfer as an act of individual cognition with the institutional realities of a specialized academy that works against the recognition and valuing of transfer. Agents of integration are individuals actively working to *perceive* as well as to *convey effectively to others* connections between previously distinct contexts.

The term *agents of integration* suggests a unit of analysis that focuses on the student's sense of self: it may be that a student feels a sense of integration, even when an external viewer might see that transfer led a student to interpret a task in ways that made the task more difficult and the final text less successful. By redirecting attention to the student's experience of transfer, the agents-of-integration construct puts the individual as meaning maker at the center of conceptions of transfer and integration.

The word *agency* emphasizes a student's ability to act and make change in the world; it also directs our attention to the social contexts in which agents operate and the standards by which they are judged. Sales agents, literary agents, secret agents: all act to accomplish their goals against some odds and perhaps against the expectations and interests of others. In this way the language of agents helpfully reminds us of a student's ability to make change, as well as the constraints that agents of integration are operating within or against. Students becoming agents of integration must learn not only to "see" connections among previously disparate contexts but also to "sell" those connections, to render them appropriate and convincing to their various audiences.

To speak of agents of integration as seers and sellers is to understand transfer as a rhetorical act: this understanding is grounded in several basic assumptions central to the idea of transfer as recontextualization elaborated in chapter 1. Because agents of integration are rhetorical actors, they seek to craft a response within an already established chain of utterances. Within that chain of utterances, there may be recurring social and rhetorical situations that give rise to genres with their associated constellations of knowledge domains, ways of knowing, identities, and goals. Inasmuch as this is true, an agent's act of seeing can be a fully conscious act, or it can be more dimly perceived, the result of tacit associations.

Grounding the concept of agents of integration in genre theory also highlights the fact that the act of selling is closely tied to the act of reading one's audience, to understanding what an audience expects and how to either meet or recalibrate that audience's expectations. Finally, the idea of agents of integration as actors within recurrent rhetorical situations emphasizes that agents' responses may be cued, but they are not predetermined. Genre is a means of production as well as interpretation; some agents reconfigure the discursive space within which they operate in order to achieve their own goals, not simply the goals articulated for them by others.

Agents of Integration and the Transfer Matrix

The term *integration*, as argued in chapter 1, implies acts of transfer that are intentional and successful. With the phrase *agents of integration*, I hope to reenvision the relations between various types of transfer. The categories of positive, negative, and zero transfer do not provide an accurate description of the lived experience of students. Instead, agents of integration operate on a spectrum—two spectra that need to be understood in relation to one another.

Figure 2.1 illustrates the relation between these two spectra by plotting a matrix of two axes. The horizontal axis plots unconscious connections on one end and meta-aware recognition of connections on the other; this is the "seeing" axis. The vertical axis plots connections that are successfully conveyed to the appropriate audience on one side, and those unsuccessfully conveyed on the other; this is the "selling" axis. The matrix as a whole accounts for both the experience of the individual perceiving the connection and the institutional context within which it is received and evaluated.

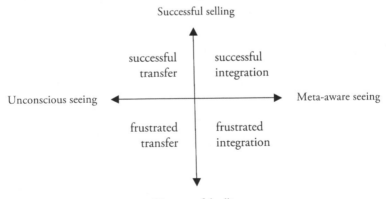

Figure 2.1. Agents of integration in the transfer matrix

Each of the quadrants of the matrix can be named, providing a more precise vocabulary to describe various acts of transfer. *Successful integration* is a term meant to describe those instances in which students consciously see a connection and successfully sell it to their audience. *Successful transfer* describes instances when a student has made a connection accepted as appropriate by the audience but has not done so with a fully conscious awareness. *Frustrated integration* describes situations in which students have consciously made a connection but fail to sell it to their audience; *frustrated transfer* describes situations in which the connection is neither consciously seen nor effectively sold.

Compared to the spectrum of meta-awareness pictured in table 1.1, this matrix does not appear to account for zero transfer—but this matrix makes visible that students aren't able to see possible connections for a variety of reasons that the concepts "negative transfer" and "zero transfer" disguise. For instance, if a student perceives, however dimly, a conflict between the expectations of two contexts, one reasonable response is to abandon that line of connection-making. Such a response should be characterized as frustrated transfer rather than zero transfer. In essence, this matrix attempts to incorporate the insights of Mikhail M. Bakhtin and Yrjo Engeström into the basic categories used to discuss transfer. My research does include instances of zero transfer in the traditional sense. In some cases, students simply do not see possible connections; in others, students may see connections but make no effort to incorporate them into their written texts or class discussions. Such instances are not, I suspect, uncommon. Any robust theory of transfer must acknowledge and account for such experiences.

When I talk with students, when I listen to them participate in class discussions, and when I read their notebooks and drafts and papers, what emerges is a portrait of individuals whose lived experience of transfer is not the all-or-nothingness suggested by the clear-cut categories of positive, negative, or zero transfer. More often than our preconceptions might predict, students feel on the cusp of bringing disparate parts of their lives together. They get excited when they sense a connection between what they are doing in one class and what they are doing in another. The flip side of this coin, though, is the very real frustration that students experience when they sense an undeveloped connection or experience a conflict between various aspects of their academic and personal lives. The pedagogical challenge is to help students develop strategies to transform these experiences of frustrated transfer into experiences of successful integration.

CONTEXT OF COURSE AND OVERVIEW OF ASSIGNMENTS

With one exception, the five students profiled in this chapter were first-year students; all were enrolled in an interdisciplinary learning community that linked their history, literature, and religious studies courses. The case studies presented here draw on my analyses of interviews with the students and teachers, analyses of student papers and notebooks, and transcripts of in-class discussions.

Each of the three professors assigned four to six writing assignments and exams during the semester (see table 0.2). Copies of the full assignments are in the appendix. Aside from coordinating due dates and general assignment types, all instructors devised and responded to their assignments independently. The assignments served primarily disciplinary (rather than interdisciplinary) goals. Yet, students did make a great many connections among the disciplines, as well as between school and extracurricular activities. In some cases, students consciously applied knowledge acquired and questions raised in one discipline to their work in another. In other cases, they found nonacademic goals and identities unexpectedly coming to the fore, reconstructing their interpretations of assignments in ways that complicated their academic work. Opportunities to integrate, for better or worse, abounded. Chapter 3 analyzes trends in student responses to these assignments, identifying assignments best able to facilitate integration.

CASE STUDIES

The diverse accounts of the five students described in these case studies demonstrate the power of the concept of agents of integration to illuminate the experience of students at different points on the transfer matrix. The experience of "Data" (a pseudonym chosen by the student) provides a relatively straightforward example of successful integration, of how seeing and selling operate within an institutional context and require rhetorical agility. The experiences of another student, Kelly, make visible the power relationships that define a given connection as positive transfer or negative transfer—as well as the inadequacies of those categories. A close reading of two papers written by Emma reveals some of the rhetorical options available to agents of integration; one is to render connections invisible within the text. Betty's experiences of transfer are informed by her identity as a non-Catholic at a Catholic university. Her experiences highlight the crucial role of students' self-constructed identities— identities that are sometimes in conflict with the identities implied by instructors' assignments—in the efforts of agents of integration to sell their connections. Finally, the example of Tygra demonstrates the central role of disciplines as both institutional and epistemological structures. Although the five principles elaborated in chapter 1 inform all of the case studies, the concepts of identity and ways of knowing as avenues of connection and of genre as an exigence for transfer become especially crucial in the last two cases.

"Data": Successfully Seeing and Selling

I invited all the students in this study to choose their own pseudonyms. That "Data" gleefully selected a name that invokes *Star Trek: The Next Generation* and comments on his status as an object of my study suggests his playful sense of humor as well as his highly developed awareness of himself as a student and a thinker. By the start of my study (during the second semester of his first year in college), Data had decided to triple major in English, economics, and honors, and minor in Spanish. He was an ambitious and accomplished member of the class, regarded by his classmates as a smart and hard-working "good guy." All three professors identified Data as a particularly successful student.

Data offers a relatively uncomplicated example of knowledge gained in one disciplinary context being transferred to another.

His experiences illustrate the processes of seeing and selling that are central to the work of agents of integration and make visible the rhetorical choices required of successful agents of integration.

Data transferred knowledge from his history course to work he did for his literature course, significantly influencing the central argument of his paper on *Doctor Faustus*. The introduction to his analysis of the significance of the low scenes in Marlowe's play shows the transfer:

> Knowledge brings power. In the Renaissance, this form of power emerged to challenge physical power, or the power of war. People such as Luther could command armies with treatises instead of swords. However, the "low" peasant or tradesman possessed neither knowledge nor power. All forms of both controlled him. His overall status had not changed greatly from the Middle Ages to the Renaissance, and as a result, knowledge, as represented by magic in *Dr. Faustus*, subjugated the "low" characters. Marlowe commented on the limited scope of the intellectual revolution, for the "lower" people plainly had not seen it, and therefore, they had not gained power.

Data's thesis hinges on a claim made in his history class. A proposition from history (the scope of the intellectual revolution was limited—affecting only 10 percent of the population) directly influenced and made possible the proposition he argued in his literature paper (through the low characters, Marlowe is commenting on the limited scope of the intellectual revolution). Because it served a central role in helping Data to generate his thesis, this act of transfer is best understood not as a matter of simple application; it is instead a more complex act of transfer-as-reconstruction, one that provided not just a brick but the entire blueprint for his argument.

Data was very conscious of this connection; he could *see* it quite clearly. When I asked Data "what guided him" as he wrote the paper, he identified class discussions as key to his invention process: "We mentioned it once or twice before in [history] class that the Renaissance only affected 10 percent of the people or whatever, and that set me off. If I hadn't heard that, I would have had no idea how much the Renaissance affected people. Therefore I would have had to pick a different thesis." Data consciously recognized the potential connection and intentionally transferred historical claims about the scope of the Reformation's intellectual revolution to guide his analysis of *Doctor Faustus*; he acted as an agent of integration. However, Data did very little to *sell* this particular connection. In fact, the connection becomes nearly invisible, recognizable only to someone who had been present during Data's history class.

The relative invisibility of this act of reconstruction offers a striking contrast to a second, more visible moment of integration in the opening paragraph: Data's reference to Martin Luther. Data explained that he had included this reference in an attempt to support his underlying assumption that knowledge equals power:

> My greatest fear was that [the literature professor] was going to question one of my assumptions which my whole paper was based on, which was knowledge equals power. . . . But I threw in one example at the very beginning. My first line was knowledge brings power and that Luther had power to split up an entire nation because he had the knowledge of, he had faith in that. So hopefully that was enough.

Again, Data acts as an agent of integration, intentionally transferring knowledge acquired in other courses to support the assumptions underlying the thesis of his literature paper. Here, though, the act of transfer is one of application: Data uses factual knowledge from his history class to provide support for the claim that knowledge equals power. This is an important and valuable instance of transfer—but it is qualitatively different from the reconstructive transfer characterized by his process of developing a thesis.

Data makes this connection visible in his text, mentioning Luther by name, but does little work to sell this connection. Nevertheless, these appear to be successful instances of integration: the paper earned an A-. The success of these two "unsold" acts of transfer might seem to suggest that agents of integration don't really need to sell their connections. On the contrary, though, these examples make visible the importance of institutional context in the process of selling. Data enjoyed the benefits of an unusual institutional context: he was enrolled in an interdisciplinary learning community that, to some considerable extent, was able to do the work of selling the connection, making it appear relevant and appropriate, for him. Data could see the connection between the literature and history claims, and (thanks to the structure of Interdisc) so could Data's professor.

It is easy to imagine a scenario in which Data's literature class was *not* linked to his history class, in which therefore the literature professor would have been unconvinced by a claim that seemed to come from nowhere with no supporting evidence. Data's exception confirms the rule: confronted with an audience of instructors who haven't participated in all the same discussions and don't see the same connections, agents of integration are regularly and by necessity put in the position of having to sell their connections.

In Data's case, integration of material across disciplinary boundaries proved an important and beneficial part of his paper; it is an uncomplicated instance of successful integration that begins to unpack the intellectual and rhetorical abilities required to successfully incorporate such connections into a paper.

Kelly: Complicating Negative Transfer

Kelly was not, by her own admission, the overachiever that many of her classmates were. She was a bright and self-aware person in the process of working out her own values and self-identity. Kelly had applied to the Honors Program only at the urgings of her parents and siblings; she initially resisted the idea of Interdisc because she didn't want to "know just twelve people in college" and didn't want to study all the time. When I asked her (as I did all students) at the end of the semester what she'd do differently if given the chance, she said that she might have done more of the readings and worked harder on the papers throughout the semester. But she also affirmed her decision to worry less about her academic work and expand her social horizons.

Some readers (or instructors) might be tempted to dismiss the challenges Kelly faced as the result of her not caring or working hard enough. But a nuanced understanding of Kelly, of her work and her development as an individual, encourages a move beyond the polarities of a theory that posits a simple division between positive transfer and negative transfer, between all or nothing. Kelly makes evident the need for a conceptual framework that will acknowledge and account for the phenomenon of transfer as experienced not just by the brightest or hardest-working students but by all students.

Kelly did work, and she did care. She simply didn't work to her full potential and for reasons that were not unreasonable. She was eighteen years old and wanted to immerse herself in things other than books. And although she may not have valued her schoolwork above all else, she did value her experience in Interdisc a great deal: she often talked about how much she enjoyed the course, respected her professors, and genuinely liked her classmates.

Kelly's experience writing a medieval diary for her history class provides an example of what in other contexts might be described as negative transfer and what I redefine as frustrated integration. The medieval-diary assignment asked students to "assume a specific medieval identity in terms of gender, age, social position, and occupation and write a diary entry for a single day." The entry "should focus on material details like what you do and where you do it, including physical surroundings, tools, who else is present, etc." Roger, the history professor, explained that this assignment was meant to focus students' attention on the lived, material reality that undergirded the "big ideas" students were discussing in their religious studies class. Papers that earned A's consistently emphasized physical, material details. However, inspired by her reading of Chaucer's portrait of the Prioress and other religious figures, Kelly composed a more psychological portrait.

Describing her invention process for the medieval diary, Kelly said she "pretty much went through *The Canterbury Tales* and tried to pick a character. I made myself a nun. But I wasn't a really, really good nun—like the Prioress. I was good, but I was more concerned with how I became a nun." As she continued, Kelly spoke with some evident pride about how she drew material from both *The Canterbury Tales* and a secondary historical text.

Although in interviews Kelly focused on the generative experience of having read *The Canterbury Tales*, it also seems probable that Kelly's inclination to take a more psychological approach, focused on feelings and motivations, may have been cued by her understanding of the genre of "diary." Genre is not the *only* exigence for transfer; in this case, transfer was also cued by the chronological and thematic overlaps between the medieval-diary assignment and Kelly's reading of Chaucer. But the possibility of writing as a nun preoccupied with how she had become a nun would likely have resonated with goals and identities commonly associated with the genre of diary: reflective, focused on emotions as well as thoughts, and personal.

Kelly operated as an agent of integration, intentionally using materials she had studied in one context to assist her invention process in another: this kind of transfer is exactly what is called for in the scholarship on integration. But Kelly did not do terribly well on this assignment, in large part *directly because of* the information she transferred from *The Canterbury Tales*. She was able to see the connections but not to sell them. Roger's endnote comment commends Kelly's diary as an "interesting psychological piece" but notes that it "could have been enhanced with more physical detail"; consequently, she received a comparatively low grade. The psychological focus that Kelly adopted from her reading of *The Canterbury Tales* (and perhaps from associations with the genre of diary) resulted in a lower grade.

However, to define Kelly's experience as negative transfer is to accept the professor's grade as the final arbiter of what counts as transfer. There are other ways to assess its value. Although this act of transfer resulted in a lower grade, it was also a tool of invention; this act of transfer helped Kelly to come up with a focus and arguably taught her something significant about vocation and station, concepts discussed in all three classes. Furthermore, it pleased Kelly to feel that work she had done in one discipline could inform work she did in another. To be sure, Kelly did not fully succeed as an agent of integration: although she saw the connections, she seemed not to be fully aware of the ways in which she needed (or, perhaps more accurately, would be unable) to sell the appropriateness of these connections for this particular assignment. As a result, Kelly's work on the medieval diary is an instance of "frustrated integration."

Exactly how much meta-awareness Kelly brought to seeing and selling the connections between her two courses remains uncertain. What is clear is that professors have the power to determine what counts as successful transfer. This example should also make clear that professors are not unkind people playing arbitrary "gotcha" games with students. They are human beings with limited knowledge and with disciplinary training. Institutional context very definitely matters, for it can have a significant influence on the professors who have the power to decide what kinds of transfer count. It may be that a more integrated curriculum will increase the likelihood of students making connections; it is almost certain that moving to a more intentionally and closely integrated curriculum will increase the likelihood of instructors recognizing such connections. Institutional context and experiences will make some connections more readily visible and acceptable to instructors.

Institutional context also matters for students. Being enrolled in an interdisciplinary learning community affected Kelly's work in and experience of her disciplinary courses. Reflecting on her *Doctor Faustus* paper, Kelly mentioned that because she had read the play in high school and focused on Faustus as a tragic hero, she would not have thought of the topic of power in *Doctor Faustus* on her own. Her current work on *Doctor Faustus* was recontextualized within, and very nearly limited by, her previous experiences. Her prior experiences might easily have led her to write on Faustus as tragic hero, merely recycling in a new context what she had already written in an earlier context. But when the assignment prompted her to consider the topic of power, she reported finding the new focus surprisingly "easy, just because . . . we talked about it so much." Kelly reflected on her experience of integration in Interdisc:

> I notice . . . we incorporate the other things we've read in all the disciplines. And I think that was probably a big part of [my ability to write on power in *Doctor Faustus*]. You know, how do you see this model of power, think about all the disciplines not just literature.

The experience of participating in a learning community affected Kelly's ability to recognize possible connections among the disciplines, making visible more opportunities for transfer.

The power of Interdisc, according to Kelly, went beyond her work on the *Doctor Faustus* paper. The knowledge she was acquiring in Interdisc had staying power. Kelly attributed this to the way professors

> would always kind of draw parallels. I finally feel like I've really learned something. In high school, it wasn't like you really learned anything. You were always cramming to remember it for the final exam. And it wasn't like that [in Interdisc]. I had to review, had to study, but . . . I feel like I could go home and watch *Jeopardy!* and if "Old Testament Theology" comes up, I would know it. And that makes me so happy! And at home when I would talk to other people and they would make a reference, [I could say]—wow, you know, Plato thought that same thing. And they were like "wow!" I know that stuff. And that's the best thing. Even now I can pretty much remember. So it definitely had an impact on me as far as retaining stuff.

That this praise comes from a student who sometimes experienced "negative" transfer—whose efforts on the medieval diary, for example, were frustrated—affirms the need to understand students as agents of integration. Seeing transfer as an experience that can be plotted on a matrix of seeing and selling and recognizing the implicit role of power relations makes visible significant variations in experience too often elided by other conceptions of transfer.

Emma: Strategies of Selling

Kelly's and Data's experiences illuminate the power relations that require students to sell connections. Emma's experiences help to clarify the circumstances under which students feel obligated to sell their connections and the strategies they might use.

Emma's future plans were vague, but she imagined a major in communications, perhaps with a focus on advertising media. Emma was relatively quiet during class but filled her notebooks with careful notes and artistic doodles. In interviews, she demonstrated a quick smile and a sense of humor that were visible, if somewhat less often, during class discussions. She excelled on her literature papers, where her clear prose and attention to detail served her well.

In a history paper responding to Robert Darnton's *Great Cat Massacre*, Emma focused on a proposition originally raised in literature class, regarding the relationship between texts and history. Over a month earlier, the literature professor had asked students to provide verbs for three sentences: "Writing _____ history; literature _____ history; history _____ writing." On that occasion, students debated what types of texts would provide future historians with the most accurate portrait of late-twentieth-century American society: experimental novels by "high culture" authors, popular novels, or other less "literary" texts. In her history paper, Emma made a subtle allusion to that prior discussion:

> The way that historians can extract a sense of eighteenth-century France through content analysis [of fairy tales] is pretty neat. Darnton tells how a "particular ethos and worldview" can be communicated by a tone of discourse or a cultural style. *... Darnton is quick to counter that these French tales cannot be depended on as single sources because they cannot escape the fact that they are fiction.* (emphasis added)

Elsewhere in her paper, Emma wrote of her frustration that "so many of the tales are rejected from 'scientific' study of the culture because of their 'unreliability.'"

The text I have italicized and Emma's explanation of her frustration can certainly be seen as a rejoinder to the earlier debate over whether literary texts can be used as historical evidence. The allusion is subtle, but because Emma knew her professor was present during that animated discussion, she could reasonably presuppose his knowledge of the connection and its appropriateness. Alternatively, it could be argued that this sentence effectively disguises any connection back to the literature conversation: grounded as it is in Darnton's claim (that "tales cannot be depended on as sources"), this subtle allusion to a connection can also stand on its own. Even without being contextualized within prior discussion, this sentence makes sense. In short, the process of selling a connection involves either disguising the connection entirely or (if the connection is made visible) justifying the appropriateness of the connection. Although I have no evidence to determine exactly how conscious this connection was for Emma, it seems likely that Emma herself saw the connection. She does almost nothing, though, to sell the connection—or even to make it visible to her professor. Perhaps she was relying on their shared classroom experience or perhaps it was so dimly perceived that she had no awareness that there was a connection that needed to be sold. Emma's level of meta-awareness is significant because in most institutional contexts her professor would have no knowledge of that discussion. Under such circumstances, Emma's choice to either disguise or more effectively justify the connection would become crucial. Without meta-awareness of both the connection and the need to sell it, a student seems far less likely to sell the connection effectively. The effectiveness of this connection seems to consist either of its invisibility or an interdisciplinary institutional experience shared by student and instructor. Either path can be effective, but in most cases only one is truly viable—thus the importance of agents of integration recognizing the need to sell their connections.

In contrast stands Emma's work on her final literature paper comparing *The Merchant of Venice* and *Paradise Lost*. Like Data, Emma's thesis for her literature paper was significantly shaped by knowledge associated with another class. When Emma chose one of the suggested topics ("compare the versions of marriage in *The Merchant of Venice* and *Paradise Lost*"), she also elected to use Thomas Hobbes (whose *Leviathan* the class had read in religious studies) as a framework for analyzing marriage as a "contractual relationship." Using Hobbes's idea of the consent of the governed, who, as Emma wrote, "must willingly accept the conditions of the agreement to which they are 'bound and obliged' (*Leviathan*, XIV, p. 34)," Emma draws distinctions between the central relationships of *Merchant* and *Paradise Lost*. When I asked Emma whether this use of Hobbes in her literature paper was intentional, she answered that she hadn't begun the paper intending to make a connection between the various materials but that she had found, as she drafted out ideas, that thinking about contract from a Hobbesian perspective was easier than "using a generic contract." For Emma as for Data, the act of transfer was an act of invention, providing her with more ideas—and more specific ideas—than she would otherwise have had.

As an agent of integration, Emma was able to see the connection between Hobbes and her literary texts—and she was also able to sell it to her literature professor. Emma helped her professor recognize the connection by attributing her conception of contract to Hobbes in the paper's opening line: "Though writers of different styles and purposes, both John Milton and William Shakespeare employ a Hobbesian perspective in presenting contractual relationships." After making the connection visible to her professor, Emma might have relied on their shared Interdisc experiences to justify the connection—but she did not. Instead, she continued to explicitly sell the value of the connection, arguing (in her thesis) that the "different directions the author and playwright take with the same premise demonstrate the contrasting themes and intentions they want to convey to the reader." Emma makes the connection visible and explicitly argues for its value as a framework able to foster a more nuanced reading of literary texts. The result was an enthusiastically received paper: next to the initial mention of Hobbes, the literature professor wrote "interesting"; next to Emma's thesis, she wrote "good thesis"; and in a final endnote, the professor praised Emma's "great idea," calling her links between contract and *Paradise Lost* "provocative."

To summarize, agents of integration working to sell their connections must make a series of rhetorical choices. They must decide first whether to make the connection visible or whether to disguise it. If they choose to make it visible, they must also work to justify the value of the connection. In some cases (as in Interdisc), students may rely on a shared institutional context, but in most cases, students will need to justify the value of the connection within the text itself.

Understanding that disguising an already recognized connection when writing for a professor may be a viable and even appealing rhetorical option adds an important dimension to our understanding of how and why students show evidence of transfer in their papers. Future research could undertake a systematic textual analysis of documents that succeed or fail to sell connections to an intended audience and thereby develop a more detailed taxonomy of textual strategies. (Journet's [1993, 1999] work on the strategies of published authors writing interdisciplinary texts may provide important groundwork for such work.)

This preliminary analysis, conducted by analyzing a small group of student papers using a rich understanding of the institutional context, points out a series of basic rhetorical choices that agents of integration must make. Furthermore, Data's and Emma's experiences suggest that knowledge connections may be relatively easy to justify. The examples of Betty and Tygra suggest that connections to identities and ways of knowing and goals may prove a much tougher sell.

Betty: Recontextualizing Identities

Betty's experiences foreground the importance of identity, which must be central to any robust understanding of transfer. Selling involves a process of determining who the audience is and what the audience wants. Such work isn't conducted in a vacuum; these judgments are made from a subject position—and in the power structure of a classroom, students have to negotiate the differences between their own self-identities and the identity they feel is required to successfully appeal to their audience. Because identity affects the process of selling, it also affects how fully integrated (or frustrated) a given instance of transfer will be.

Unlike her classmates, Betty was a sophomore midyear transfer student from a secular university. She seemed to her teachers and fellow students more mature than many in the class: this may have been due to her sophomore status, but it was also a function of her confidence and keen awareness of her own thought processes. She was liked and respected by her classmates but tended to socialize outside the classroom with members of her athletic team, which consumed much of her time. Betty's experiences in Interdisc highlight the ways in which identity can be a key avenue of transfer. In particular, her identity as a non-Catholic, which was called forth by genre, significantly influenced her interpretation of task and invention process.

Betty struggled with the religious studies assignment on Thomas Aquinas. She felt the assignment presupposed and would value the identity of a good Catholic believer, someone who learns her Aquinas and defends its value. The identity Betty believed was implicitly constructed by the assignment did not easily align with the identity Betty had constructed for herself as a Quaker. As she connected these two previously disparate contexts—her identity as a student and her identity as a Quaker—Betty's religious identity began to redefine her understanding of her academic assignment; in this case, transfer as a process of reconstruction proved more of a rhetorical obstacle than a means of invention.

One of only three non-Catholic students in Interdisc, Betty was the only one to speak publicly of not being Catholic. Her religious background differed from most of her classmates', not only because she was not Catholic but also because she had changed religious affiliations. As a child, Betty had been a member of a Unitarian Universalist church, but in fifth grade, her family began attending Quaker meeting. "I really like that," Betty said, "and I definitely consider myself a Quaker."

Betty expressed little doubt about her faith but did express concern about how others perceived that faith. Her university describes itself as an institution that welcomes students of all faiths, and certainly Betty had experiences that affirmed her Quaker faith; for instance, the chair of the English department—also a Quaker—made her acquaintance and offered to bring her along to his meeting house, a gesture Betty clearly appreciated. Other experiences, however, led Betty to view the university's religious culture with some suspicion.

Thomas, her religious studies professor, became a focus of Betty's suspicion. In interview after interview, Betty made clear that although she liked her professor and thought he was a very fine teacher, she worried that he was trying to instill Catholic beliefs.

I love Thomas to death, but I look at him as really having an agenda. . . . I think it's really important to him, and I honestly think he feels that one of his jobs as a [Catholic university] theologian or faculty is . . . to instill some belief in us. I don't know, maybe I'm totally reading it wrong, but that was the impression I got.

As Betty describes her uncertainty about her professor's motives, she sees them as linked, almost inextricably, to the institutional context of her Catholic university. What troubled Betty most about the Aquinas assignment was her sense that it was designed, in her words, to "get the Catholic kids learning exactly how a very famous Catholic theologian says this is how you are saved." As Betty read the assignment, she latched on to the phrases "I want you to be his defense lawyer, get inside his head," and "I want you to make a case for the reasonableness of Aquinas's theology on this issue." The assignment does acknowledge the possibility of disagreement, and a number of Betty's classmates did include some critique. But Betty seems most influenced by those phrases that suggest that there is a party line to which successful students will adhere.

That Betty's interpretation of the assignment is influenced by the conflict she perceives between her own felt identity and the identity implied by the assignment is clear in an excerpt from a group interview conducted with Betty, Alan, and Tygra. Betty initiates the conversation by asking what the others thought of the Aquinas assignment. They respond that it was a reasonable, challenging assignment. When Tygra asks, "Did *you* not like it?" Betty quickly answers, "No, I thought it was alright," but then redirects the conversation, eventually suggesting that their professor may have a personal agenda:

> BETTY: Maybe it's because I come from a very different perspective, but [*pause*] it seemed, it seemed very like [*pause*] [the university] would like you to think this way so I'll kind of teach it that way. To me.
> TYGRA: Really?
> ALAN: I didn't see it that way at all.
> BETTY: Like, [the university] would like you to know exactly what Aquinas said, to the tee, so I'm going to make sure you get out of your theology requirement knowing this.

Tygra seems a bit flummoxed by this possibility but after mulling it over, concedes that such an agenda might be possible and attributes their different perceptions to their different religious backgrounds. "See, for me," Tygra said, "a lot of what he says is actually pretty unbiased, because I come from people pushing it down my throat more. I had seven years of Catholic school so to me he seems very not like that. But if you're a Quaker, it might seem that way."

Tygra's and Betty's interpretations of academic task—their understandings of the expectations placed upon them in their identity as student—are significantly influenced by their religious identities. While the importance of student identity and personal affiliation has long been recognized as a significant part of writing and invention (Brooke 1987; Herrington and Curtis 2000), identity has been underappreciated as an avenue for transfer. This tension between Betty's identity-as-student and identity-as-non-Catholic *is* an instance of transfer—an instance of the double bind that Engeström (1987) describes. Two contexts that are ordinarily distinct for Betty and for many students were brought into contact and conflict. She saw a conflict between her felt identity as a Quaker and her expected identity as student; unless Betty could find a way either to disconnect these two identities or to reconcile them and move forward, she risked being stuck in this space of conflict and cognitive dissonance.

Betty's double bind of conflicting identities might also be understood as embedded in a larger problem of genre. The Aquinas assignment created and invited a certain discursive space; a traditional "thesis-driven" essay defending Aquinas suggests not only certain goals (to defend Aquinas) and conventions (to articulate a strong argument and support it with specific evidence from the *Summa*) but it also implies certain associated identities (that of an individual who does in fact wish to defend Aquinas). To solve this problem, a problem caused to some degree by the genred discursive space that Betty felt she was being asked to inhabit, Betty ingeniously used genre to redefine the identity position open to her as a student-author composing a response to this assignment. In this case, we see how genres invite but do not predetermine responses.

Rather than adhering to a thesis-driven structure, Betty wrote her paper as a dialogue between Aquinas and a highly deferential student. She explained her choice:

If I'm pretending to be Aquinas, I figured that's as much in his head as I can get. And because I thought it's a logical way to explore philosophy . . . and to explore an argument and what everyone's thinking. There were a lot of parts to the paper that it was just natural for me as a student. . . . I was the student.

Abandoning the genre of thesis-driven essay for a dialogue meant that rather than having to assume the identity of committed intellectual arguing for a single position, Betty could assume a more neutral identity as author, putting all questions and answers into the mouths of others without indicting herself. What's more, because the dialogue is a genre resonant with fictional plays, it tacitly suggests these opinions might not be Betty's own but the words of a fictionalized character.

Betty did not pull this rhetorical strategy out of thin air; it was one she had used previously in a philosophy class.

What made me write a dialogue the first time was my coach helped me with the paper because I was having trouble with [a] class and he's a smart guy. . . . And I asked him for help on this paper. I just didn't know what I was doing, and he sat down with me for a few hours . . . and he was like okay, this just makes sense. Let's write a dialogue, you know, and he showed me how to do it.

Faced with a personally and rhetorically challenging situation, Betty acted as an agent of integration, consciously drawing on strategies that she associated with philosophy. This second act of integration (drawing on experiences writing philosophy papers to succeed in her religious studies class) helped her sidestep some of the difficulty generated by the first instance of transfer (a conflict between the identity implied in the assignment and her identity as Quaker). Ultimately, she received a relatively high grade on the paper.

Betty's experience illuminates the dynamic relation between identity and genre—each one able to cue the other. It also illustrates an important point: although identity is but one of the four avenues of transfer named in chapter 1's principle 1, because identity is linked to the process of reading and selling to an audience, it is particularly crucial for our understanding of agents of integration.

Tygra: Disciplinary Obstacles to Successful Transfer

Tygra's work in the Interdisc classroom illustrates how disciplinarity serves as a central system for valuing acts of transfer. Because disciplines are so vital to current constructions of the academy, it may be that some sales jobs are doomed to failure. The success of agents of integration may be limited by the institutional structures within which they work—for reasons that have less to do with a lack of connection between classes (making it difficult for students to *see* connections) and more to do with genres and their constellated associations (making it difficult for students to *sell* connections to instructors who are limited by their institutional location and disciplinary ways of knowing).

Tygra was one of the strongest and warmest personalities in the Interdisc classroom. She was smart and outspoken; she cracked jokes in class and was quick to offer hugs to classmates whose spirits were low. Her classmates frequently expressed affection for Tygra and admiration for her ability to make what one classmate described as "random connections" that later seemed like remarkable insights. Overcommitted to many different activities and organizations, Tygra was not initially going to be a focal student—but eager to make sure my research would succeed (after all, she speculated, she, too, might go to graduate school someday and need to rely on the willingness of research participants), she conducted most of her "interviews" at home, on her own, with a tape recorder and a list of questions I had written out. Apropos her sometimes offbeat sense of humor, Tygra chose her pseudonym in honor of her favorite character on her favorite cartoon show: the character of Tygra on *Thundercats*.

While writing her literature paper on *Doctor Faustus*, Tygra found herself negotiating a conflict between the identity and goals and ways of knowing implied by the literature paper assignment and her emergent identity and goals and ways of knowing as a historian. She seems in some moments to have been aware of the conflict and able to make a "metacommunicative statement" about it, but the traditional genre of "analysis essay" (discussed at length in chapter 4) provided little opportunity for Tygra to communicate her awareness to her instructor. It is possible that there was the kind of "learning by expansion" Engeström says may result from meta-awareness of a double bind; it is certain that the paper received a relatively low grade. The persistent challenges facing Tygra do not diminish the value of meta-awareness but highlight the obstacles that disciplinarily genred spaces pose to interdisciplinary integration.

Throughout her literature paper, Tygra makes claims that are in keeping with the ways of knowing valued in her history class.*

The opening paragraph of her paper on the "low" scenes in *Doctor Faustus* begins:

> Power plays a major role in *Dr. Faustus*. This is not an uncommon theme for many writings of the Middle Ages. Yet, *Dr. Faustus* is unique from others in that the struggle for power occurs not only among those of high social standing, but also among people of a lower social status. *These "low" people, in earlier writings, were never concerned about having a sense of control. In fact, the concept of control over one's life was nonexistent among the lower classes.* Marlowe's play reveals the ever increasing preoccupation with power among all classes; evidence of an evolving sense of self, not apparent in earlier writings such as *The Courtier* and *The Prince*. (emphasis added)

---

* Throughout this section, I describe Tygra as employing ways of knowing associated with history and with literature. To be clear: I am talking about instantiations of the disciplines of history and literary studies made present in this particular classroom by these particular instructors. Disciplines are complex and internally variegated social structures, and no individual instructor can be said to be fully representative of an entire discipline. Roger, for instance, cannot be said to typify all historians; at the same time, I argue (see Nowacek 2009, 502–5) that these instructors' ways of knowing—particularly their preferences for certain types of thesis claims and evidence—should not be dismissed merely as the idiosyncrasies of individual professors but are epistemological differences related to larger disciplinary trends. Chapter 3 discusses the challenges of making these epistemological differences visible to students.

In the text italicized, Tygra makes a claim very much like those made throughout the history component of the Interdisc class. Whereas the literature professor was reluctant to generalize about what other people thought, the history and religious studies professors were committed to helping students adopt a different mindset (what the religious studies professor described as "building a mental model" of how another person makes sense of the world) and were comfortable characterizing the thoughts of individuals or whole classes of individuals. It becomes clear in the way that the literature professor responds to this paragraph that she finds the interdisciplinary connection Tygra has made—her attempt to use a way of knowing valued in one discipline when writing for another—problematic.

The literature professor's objections to Tygra's approach become clear through her comments on Tygra's paper. Between the words *the* and *concept*, the literature professor inserts a caret pointing to this remark: "X [a phenomenon, or a text, or a scholar—whatever] suggests that . . . (because you need some evidence or specifics to give this assertion any authority)." She insists that Tygra's claim about the relationship between texts and material reality must be explicitly and directly grounded first in specific evidence in order to "give this assertion any authority." Such grounding was not necessary in Tygra's history class, where the professor regularly made generalizations about the premodern outlook that were not directly linked to a particular phenomenon, text, or scholar.

Whereas the literature professor would point to contradictions in a specific text and offer only tentative conclusions about what this *might* mean about a culture, the history professor would make much broader statements about the mindsets of various individuals or classes of people. Thus, when Tygra writes that "the concept of control over one's life was nonexistent among the lower classes," she tacitly draws on a proposition and employs the ways of knowing modeled in her history class. Unfortunately, by tacitly presuming this proposition and way of knowing—neither omitting nor justifying them in some way—Tygra leaves unproblematized interdisciplinary connections that exist in difficult (if not contradictory) relationships for her literature professor. As an agent of integration, Tygra sees the connections but does not effectively sell them; she does not succeed in integrating the connection in ways her literature professor would find convincing and compelling.

Other examples of Tygra using the ways of knowing and propositions associated with her history course—and the literature professor's objections to such moments—can be found throughout Tygra's paper. Next to a later claim that "the 'low' people have no fear of punishment, and no sense of modesty," the literature professor wrote, "I don't quite follow you here." Tygra's claim does not offer analysis of the textual passages she had cited in the first part of the paragraph; instead, propositions argued in history—including the "lack of modesty" of the lower classes, as well as the culturally defined nature of the concept of "modesty"—are simply assumed. Similarly, in her paper's conclusion, Tygra again draws on a proposition from history class: "[T]he goal of earning power or a rank higher than one's peers is evidence that, in general, individuals in society began to look at themselves in that way—as individuals, rather than as part of a collective group." That a premodern emphasis on the collective gave way to a modern preoccupation with the individual was a proposition argued by all three instructors but most prominently by the history professor. And when Tygra makes this claim, the evidence she offers is only secondarily textual; it is articulated as a generalization about the goals of a class of people at a certain historical moment—once again making her claim in ways consonant with what was modeled in history rather than literature.

Why is it that Tygra can see the connections but does not effectively sell them? One possible answer is that she lacks sufficient meta-awareness of the differences between the genres and of the rhetorical situation facing her. However, evidence from drafts and interviews suggest that Tygra could articulate some significant differences between these two ways of knowing. Although she was aware of her literature professor's affinity for claims grounded in textual evidence, Tygra was more concerned with one of the arguments the history professor had been making: namely, that the modern perspective differs significantly from the premodern view of the world:

> She [the literature professor] is real into this language thing I notice. This is the second time when she wants us to draw some kind of implications from the actual words in the play, which I think sometimes is a little stupid because we know very little about the time period and we're drawing with our own modern conceptions.

Here, Tygra questions the value of textual analysis because she fears her analyses will be tainted by her own modern perspective, which, as the history professor repeatedly argued, is different from the pre-modern perspective.

It seems possible that Tygra was aware of this conflict between ways of knowing but chose to align herself and her text with the disciplinary approach that made the most sense to her. Whatever the extent of Tygra's meta-awareness (she recognizes that the literature professor is "real into this language thing" but thinks such an approach may sometimes be "a little stupid"), the ways of knowing characteristic of her history and literature classes were not easy to reconcile. Although she may have sensed a conflict, she did not appear to have the textual or epistemological ability to successfully mediate the conflict and sell history ways of knowing within her literature paper.

In many ways, Tygra would seem to have been ideally positioned for success: she was an intelligent, meta-aware student enrolled in an interdisciplinary learning community. Some readers might blame Tygra's professor—but that would be unfair. The connections and missed opportunities that I hope to make clear for a reader of this chapter were not obvious to participants in this classroom: the connections only became clear to me as a researcher after I had spent many hours with drafts and transcripts.

Nor is the fault Tygra's. Tygra was working against powerful institutional and epistemological imperatives to keep two disciplines distinct. Thomas Bender's (1993) historical analyses of the emergence of the modern university system suggest that its increasing specialization is deeply rooted in historical trends (including a shift from a model of intellectualism centered in the life of a city to the more professionalized model of the German-style university) that no individual is likely to buck. Under such circumstances, success would have required not only metacognitive awareness but also an extraordinary level of rhetorical dexterity. In truth, it may be that within her literature paper, Tygra had relatively few options to help her sell the use of history ways of knowing. How might she have structured her argument, textually or rhetorically? How could she sell connections that basically supplant the ways of knowing valued by her literature professor?

What Tygra's example highlights is *not* the failure of a student ("if only she had been more aware"), a teacher ("if only she had noticed Tygra's connections"), or even a curriculum ("if only the courses had been more intentionally integrated"). Tygra's example suggests that although we quite rightly recognize transfer as an act of cognition made by individual students (an act that can be prompted and supported by thoughtful teachers and curriculum design), we make a grave mistake if we do not recognize the broader institutional and epistemological contexts in which students recontextualize their knowledge. It is hard for students to make the connections and potentially harder yet for teachers to see and value those connections.

So does this mean transfer is impossible, that agents of integration are doomed to failure? No. These cases suggest that if instructors want to teach for transfer, it is not enough to change the curriculum by linking classes; instructors must intentionally work to defamiliarize and make more pliable the genred discursive spaces within which students see and sell connections—and in which instructors recognize those connections.

If instructors want to see more instances of transfer in student work, they will need to work with richer definitions of transfer that do not reduce transfer to the simple application of content knowledge or a bullet-pointed writing "skill"; instructors will need definitions that recognize the full rhetorical complexity of the task facing agents of integration involved in the process of seeing and selling. More particularly, they will need to develop written and spoken genres that allow students to inhabit identities, employ ways of knowing, and pursue goals that link these different disciplines. These more pliable discursive spaces might allow instructors to perceive the connections more readily as well. I do not mean to suggest that interdisciplinary connections are impossible within traditional disciplinary genres. However, because disciplinary epistemologies are deeply intertwined with classroom genres of writing and talking, helping students and instructors to recognize, challenge, and reshape those discursive spaces becomes a crucial element of teaching for transfer.

CONCLUSION

By way of conclusion, I return to the questions posed at the start of this chapter: How do institutional structures affect student and instructor perceptions of transfer? And what are the capacities that students develop in order to become agents of integration?

Individually and cumulatively, these five case studies provide compelling evidence for the significant effect of institutional context on transfer. Viewing students as agents of integration brings into focus the ways in which institutional context strongly influences students' abilities to draw connections. Transfer is an act of individual cognition but one that is often made possible in ways both conscious and unconscious by the genred discursive spaces of the classroom. The concept of agents of integration also highlights the ways in which the term *negative transfer* normalizes and renders largely invisible the power differentials that determine the value of any given instance of transfer. Although students may perceive a connection, they do not generally get to determine its worth.

That job is left for instructors—and instructors, too, are affected by institutional contexts. Some connections remain unseen because the curricular divisions between classes work against an instructor's ability to recognize a seemingly random reference or claim as a response meaningful within another chain of utterances. In other cases, disciplinary inclinations toward certain epistemologies impede instructors' abilities to perceive and value some of the many instances of transfer that are already in student work.

As for student capacities, these examples suggest that a savvy agent of integration sees transfer as a rhetorical act. One capacity that successful agents of integration must develop is the ability to forge connections; genres can help individuals see such connections. Another is the ability to read an audience and find a way of making connections seem appropriate to that audience. Agents of integration may sometimes perceive a connection but choose to omit it from the text, knowing it would not be valued.

These cases also point toward a more general implication for instruction. Genre serves as an important exigence for transfer—but in some cases, transfer can serve as the exigence for new genres. Genred discursive spaces—that is, the constellation of associations attached to a given genre (like the diary)—may help students to *see* connections. But when faced with the task of *selling* connections, agents of integration may be pressed to experiment with different genred responses. Among the students in this study, the conscious reconfiguring of genred discursive space happens very rarely; Betty provides the only clear example. It seems likely that an inclination and ability to reconfigure the genred discursive space are linked to a conscious understanding of the need to sell a connection to a potentially resistant audience. If a student remains largely unaware of the need to sell the connection, then that student's sense of opportunities will be limited to the tacit associations of the current genres.

Herein, then, lies the real opportunity for instructors to teach for transfer—by shaping new genred discursive spaces. Chapter 3 turns to examples of such attempts.

3

Agents, Handlers, Audience Members: The Challenges Facing Instructors Teaching for Transfer

Everything is so intertwined, all three subjects. Like when we'd discuss a subject in one class, it would come up in all the other ones, and we could see how every part of society was affected by things.

—Henry

The best thing we did was read about Luther in Roger's [history] class and then read what he wrote in Thomas's [religious studies] class. That's the best thing I ever did. When I read [Luther in religious studies], I would have had no clue otherwise. I think about it a lot actually.

—Tygra

THESE ARE TWO OF MANY TESTIMONIALS offered by students praising the integrated nature of Interdisc. Students' experiences of the course were, by and large, that of a closely interwoven learning community that helped them examine ideas and texts from multiple perspectives. When a student asked how much the overlaps were planned and how much they "just happened," Roger explained:

No, it's more than just accident. [T]he first time the three of us taught [together], each of us came up with a list of topics for the semester. And then we spent a fair amount of time juggling them around, so that things that could relate would relate. . . . So we're pleased you noticed.

Teaching for transfer within Interdisc II, Roger explained, builds on a foundation established by the coordinated syllabi. But the actual lived experience of Interdisc—students' feelings that "everything is so intertwined," that reading Luther in history and religious studies was "the best thing I ever did"—is determined not only by a sequence of readings but also by the daily interactions among students and teachers. Such interactions, mediated by spoken and written classroom genres, make transfer possible.

Chapter 2 describes students as agents of integration, working to sell their connections to instructors who have the institutional authority to decide which connections count. This chapter focuses on instructors who, when teaching for transfer, shift among a complex trio of roles. Instructors may function as agents of integration themselves, seeing and selling connections. Instructors may also function (in an extension of the "agent" metaphor) as the agents' "handlers"—working behind the scenes through assignment prompts and class discussions to promote the success of students-as-agents. Finally, instructors may also function as the audience to whom students must sell their connections.

This chapter focuses on the ways in which genres—with their constellations of associated knowledge domains, ways of knowing, identities, and goals—affect transfer for teachers. What are the exigencies and constraints that classroom genres, both spoken and written, provide to instructors teaching for transfer? In their capacity as handlers, instructors can encourage or require certain spoken and written genres. Some genres are more pliable and therefore encourage students to make connections; other genres, as the case of Tygra in chapter 2 suggests, make it difficult for students to make connections visible—making it difficult to sell connections to an audience. However, in their capacity as agents and even audience members, instructors' abilities to see and sell connections are often impeded by genres—in particular by spoken and written genres that serve to keep the rhetorical dimensions of disciplines invisible.

INSTRUCTORS AS AGENTS: THE CHALLENGES OF TEACHING FOR TRANSFER ACROSS DISCIPLINES

Like students, instructors in their capacity as agents operate within institutional contexts, where disciplinary training and expectations work against the impulse to draw connections. Making visible and selling connections to students who do not yet understand disciplines as disciplines poses challenges. How these challenges manifest within day-to-day classroom practice and how instructors-as-agents might overcome them are best illustrated by Thomas's and Olivia's efforts to teach for transfer.

Although Thomas, Roger, and Olivia recognized the potential to emphasize disciplinary differences, they chose to focus on what they described as "convergences" and "linkages." To do so, the Interdisc professors needed to invoke or create genres of talk and writing that encouraged students to see links that might otherwise be hidden or ignored. Genres are a "stabilized-for-now," typified response to a recurring rhetorical exigence; one important recurring exigence in the Interdisc classroom was the task of sorting out how multiple professors would interact.

Each Interdisc professor favored a different mode of integration, embodied a distinct approach to seeing and selling connections. Roger most often engaged in what he described as "super-student" mode—asking questions to encourage his fellow instructors to make connections or explain things more fully (e.g., "Yesterday we were talking about civic virtue and what it means to be a good citizen. Is that the same as what you're saying about [*Dangerous Liaisons*]?"). Olivia often stepped up (sometimes literally getting up and joining another instructor at the board) to coteach or even debate with fellow instructors, taking on the role of "interdisciplinary gadfly." Thomas's most frequent mode of participating in others' classes was as "resident expert." Implicit in each of these modes of integration are different goals, different instructor identities, different relationships to the idea of disciplinary ways of knowing; each mode of integration, in short, creates a genred discursive space through which participants both interpret and cocreate the connections between disciplines.

The genred discursive space that constitutes and is constituted by each is strikingly different: each approach has different goals and promotes significantly different patterns of class discussion. Students' legacies of schooling (particularly their understanding of disciplines and the antecedent genres they use to interpret and construct their classroom) affect student receptivity to various approaches. Especially instructive is the contrast between the resident expert and interdisciplinary gadfly approaches; most Interdisc students embraced the former and resisted the latter.

Connecting Subjects: Agent of Integration as "Resident Expert"

Thomas's decision to stress convergences was a principled one. Very few first-year students, he explains, have developed a rich understanding of disciplines; instead, they attribute disciplinary differences to personalities:

> I'm not sure that they can separate us as people from what we do: what is it that Thomas does and what is it that's Thomas. Until they get another somebody like me to make a comparison, figuring out what the disciplinary differences are becomes a real problem. . . . And I'm just not sure as freshmen they've had enough exposure at the college level to really put flesh and bones on the concept of discipline.

Most first-year students think not of disciplines but of academic subjects, defined primarily by their content and perhaps also by the personalities and teaching methods of the instructors students have encountered. Thomas suggests that only over time do students begin to understand subjects as disciplines.

Thomas's view of students' intellectual development is borne out by research into the nature of disciplinary expertise. Cheryl Geisler (1994) argues that students are introduced to the knowledge domains (or "facts") of disciplines but given little opportunity to recognize, much less participate in, the rhetorical domains of that expertise (the ways in which disciplinary knowledge is created, disputed, and accorded status as fact). David R. Russell and Arturo Yañez (2003) document a similar divide. Only as students move beyond general education classes, Geisler argues, is the curtain drawn back to show the rhetorical processes—the ways of knowing, the sense of making an argument to a community of scholars—that guide expert work. The institutional reality is that most first-year students are in the cognitive position Thomas describes.

Given this reality, Thomas put his efforts toward helping students make knowledge connections. His goal as an agent of integration was to help students to see the many possible connections among their various subjects. This approach, Thomas explains, offers students a rare counterpoint to their usual fragmented experience of the curriculum. To achieve this ambitious goal required the kind of coordinated syllabi that Roger described at the start of this chapter, as well as a major time commitment from Thomas—both to attend his colleagues' class sessions and to explore those connections with students.

The goal of drawing knowledge connections led Thomas to interpret and create the genred discursive space of the classroom as one that valued disciplinary expertise but did not explore the rhetorical domains of that expertise. He would sometimes take time at the start of his own class—which most often incorporated periods of prepared lecture as well as stretches during which he answered questions, basic and complex, from the students—to make connections back to content or propositions raised in other professors' classes. Similarly, Thomas would participate in his co-instructors' classes in the mode of resident expert. For instance, during a literature class on Francis Bacon's notion of the idols of the mind, Thomas entered the conversation at various points to answer questions and draw connections to religious studies, including a connection to John Calvin.

> THOMAS: This whole approach of Bacon to idols of the mind? It's just taking Calvin out of religion and putting him into science. . . . Calvin is obsessed with idols. And they're idols of the mind. And what they are is our conceptions imposed upon God—otherwise known as Catholic conceptions imposed upon God. The mind making up its own gods, which are then user-friendly, smaller, and very misleading. And what Bacon is doing, in a way, is saying, well, you gotta get rid of those idols, get rid of that Catholic tradition, and go to the source of truth. That is the second bible.

ROGER: It's interesting because going back, of course, it was also idols—that was how the Spanish characterized what was evil about the Maya.

THOMAS: Mm-hmm.

ROGER: Was going for those idols.

In this excerpt, all three instructors worked to make visible and sell connections among the content of the various subjects by clearly spelling them out for students: Bacon (studied in literature class) is linked to Calvin (studied in theology class) and to the Spanish conquests (studied in history class).

Resident experts draw connections on the level of knowledge rather than ways of knowing by participating in their traditional identities as knowledge providers. Resident experts connect the dots between the subjects (the theology professor enters into the literature discussion to speak of Calvin, the history professor to speak of the Maya) without exploring the nature of the boundaries between them in any fundamental way.

The resident-expert mode, with all its attendant associations—no visible ways of knowing, a clear and authoritative instructor identity, the goal to make commonalities clear—was an especially successful means of making connections visible and selling them to students. The students frequently praised how integrated the class was, how often they saw connections among their work for the history, literature, and religious studies components.

This approach also has its hazards, for the more closely instructors work to connect subjects, the more likely they are to butt up against disciplinary differences. This became evident during a discussion of John Donne's Holy Sonnets, led cooperatively by Thomas and Olivia. The two professors never engaged each other directly as interlocutors; instead, each took turns, in an apparently impromptu fashion, leading discussion. Using the Holy Sonnets as an object of simultaneous and interwoven study established strong connections between the two disciplines. For example, students worked through the lexicon of sonnet 14 with Olivia, then "translated" those images into theological terms with Thomas.

But the limitations of this approach were made evident in the way a classroom of usually gregarious students struggled to keep pace with the very different interpretive approaches of their instructors. (Both students and teachers recalled this class period as particularly "dead.") Observing the class was like watching a tennis match: questions assuming no certainty of authorial intent, generating a range of possible interpretations from one side of the table; questions assuming authorial intent and "translating" the meaning of the poem from the other. Students may have made connections on the level of content, but they were also butting up against differences in ways of knowing, of how to read and make sense of a text. To use Yrjo Engeström's language, the double bind was never subject to a metacommunicative statement, for the resident-expert mode of integration never acknowledges differences among ways of knowing.

Despite this occasional shortcoming, the resident-expert mode remained an effective approach to selling connections to students. Why? This approach to integration validates students' current, non-rhetorical understanding of disciplinary expertise. For students who perceive their different classes as subjects rather than disciplines— who recognize knowledge domains but not rhetorical domains— knowledge connections make sense and are, in fact, the only connections they'd expect to encounter.

The resident-expert mode also fits easily with students' classroom genre expectations. Most of the Interdisc II students had been in Interdisc I and brought expectations from that course that led them to embrace the resident-expert mode. As a resident expert, Thomas was knowledgeable, and although he reached across disciplinary boundaries, he appeared to respect, even embody, disciplinary expertise; he provided students with clear information on complicated subjects, inspiring their confidence. One student described Thomas as "the teacher of the teachers." In his capacity as disciplinary expert, Thomas frequently and explicitly helped students see how the content and the propositions argued in his discipline intersected with the knowledge domains of history and literature.

Thomas's resident expert approach—and students' enthusiasm for it—illustrate the degree to which the success of teachers' efforts to sell connections to students rests on a paradox: to reach across disciplinary boundaries, an instructor can't give up too much disciplinary authority. The knowledge connections made by resident experts are readily saleable to students, but to connect ways of knowing would be to make visible the rhetorical domain of disciplinary expertise—an act that can make all disciplinary expertise appear conditional and contingent. This is the challenge facing the interdisciplinary gadfly.

Connecting Disciplines: Agent of Integration as "Interdisciplinary Gadfly"

Olivia's commitment to highlighting connections was visible in acts large and small. Hers was the only assignment to explicitly encourage connections, and she frequently asked students to journal about literature texts in light of materials they had studied in other disciplines. She also attended to the subtle-but-powerful effects of material conditions upon students' willingness to forge connections across disciplines:

> Last year we let the space considerations push the people that weren't actually teaching out onto the edge [of the classroom]. Then at times Roger and I would explicitly both sit next to each other at the table because we were both really coteaching the same text, like history of science stuff. I wanted that to happen more. And I also had Roger reorganize the syllabus so it's less disciplinarily separated. . . . Because last year we thought students were not making the kinds of connections they need to be. So I wanted to find little ways to chip away at that.

Olivia also sought to transform the ways students saw their classes, to recognize their school subjects as academic disciplines. Toward this end, Olivia worked as an agent of integration by engaging her fellow instructors in conversations about ways of knowing and debates about their differences—a mode of integration I term the "interdisciplinary gadfly."

Talking about epistemological differences in front of students is potentially perilous. For teachers, disciplinary ways of knowing are so deeply engrained that they become "natural" and seem inevitable. For students, the challenge is to distinguish the merely idiosyncratic from the epistemological: as Thomas observes, until students take a number of classes in a single discipline, they can find it difficult to "separate us as people from what we do." (Thaiss and Zawacki [2006] trace a similar trajectory of disciplinary understanding.) Furthermore, when ways of knowing conflict, students—and instructors, too—can feel the need to determine which approach is better. In addition, disagreement might be mistaken for an interpersonal failing rather than an epistemological conflict. The temptation, documented by Pamela Grossman, Samuel Wineburg, and Stephen Woolworth (2001), is to revert to pseudocommunity, to brush over such differences in an effort to get along.

The challenges of making connections among different ways of knowing are suggested by the following example. Roger had been lecturing on the causes and effects of the scientific revolution, when Olivia raised her hand:

OLIVIA: Can we have an argument?

ROGER: Sure.

OLIVIA: Are you finished with what you're doing?

ROGER: Yes.

OLIVIA: I want to try a different story on you. There's no such thing as a scientific revolution. That is a paradigm cooked up in hindsight to valorize the interests of nineteenth- and twentieth-century people. The most important practices of the so-called scientific method were already in place. . . . The scientific revolution isn't a revolution, because the same kinds of practices keep going on. Tons of people don't even know this has happened. You know, you're down on your farm: what revolution? And even the guys who are on the forefront of this so-called revolution, like Bacon and Boyle? When you look at what they're *actually* doing, as opposed to what they *say* they're doing, they're not following any of the methods that they cook up either. So what revolution, right?

ROGER: Okay, ah, I agree with you on method. The scientific method has always been overrated. . . . Even in the twentieth century, there are some biographies that suggest that major breakthroughs with genes and stuff is really more of an intuition than the scientific method. But I would say it remains important, falling back on revolution, for two reasons. First of all, because it has this enormous impact on the whole philosophical structure of the sciences. In some way, what's most important is that the philosophy that comes out of it—with people like Bacon and Descartes—changed the way people saw the world. . . . Secondly, it has enormous impact upon the West because, in effect, if something happens that a whole lot of people think is important, then it *is* [important], if only because a lot of people *think* it is. And certainly the whole notion of the Enlightenment and human progress used the notion of the scientific revolution as its base. So even if it's the myth of what happened, it's important because people believed it happened.

OLIVIA: Oh, I don't know that so many people thought it was important. And the Enlightenment emphasizes far more reason and natural ability of each person.

ROGER: I think, because the change in how we think has already happened, that I would say the crucial thing that happens in science is the big divide between religious faith and knowledge of physical causes.

OLIVIA: Okay, in Paris and London—but what about in the villages where everybody else is?

In this exchange, Olivia and Roger articulate different epistemological approaches to understanding the scientific revolution and to writing history. They debate what counts as evidence for an intellectual revolution: a powerful explanatory paradigm developed by historians or the lived experience of contemporary non-elites. Throughout the semester, Roger's "intellectual history" approach traced the changing mindsets of individuals and civilizations. Olivia's approach to the writing of history, perhaps influenced by cultural materialism within literary studies, turned to different explanatory paradigms and sources of evidence. Although this conflict of theoretical approaches does not line up neatly along clear disciplinary boundaries (i.e., literary analyses can take an intellectual history approach, historians can adopt a cultural materialist approach), Olivia and Roger's exchange did manifest an epistemological conflict in the classroom.

The real challenge for professors-as-agents operating in the interdisciplinary-gadfly mode is to create a discursive space in which epistemological disagreement is not conflated with being personally disagreeable. The challenge is especially acute when instructors are attempting to make such contrasts visible to students who have little-to-no sense of the rhetorical domains of their studies, who see subjects rather than disciplines and personal idiosyncrasies rather than epistemological differences.

Olivia, Roger, and Thomas recalled the scientific revolution exchange in particular, and other instances like it, when describing the kind of work they wanted to do in Interdisc. They paced their syllabi to create such intellectual overlaps; they attended each other's classes to provide moments to coteach. Olivia identified this very moment as an example of what the Interdisc instructors strive for.

Students, however, took a very different view of such moments—focusing on conflict and inappropriate behavior. When I met with the students in a focus group, Henry offered an unprompted recollection of the scientific revolution discussion:

HENRY: I'll be honest about this. [Remember the day] when Olivia kind of criticized Roger about the scientific revolution? I don't know if it was supposed to help us in terms of understanding whether there was a scientific revolution or not. But she was like, "Well, Roger, *was* there a scientific revolution? What's the deal?" And I found that kind of annoying, unnecessary almost.

KELLY: I found that incredibly irritating.

HENRY: I didn't know if she was trying to clarify for us—but I don't think that was the purpose of his lecture. It was to teach us the mindset and the change in the mindset during that time. And her theory was, "Well, there was

no change in mindset," and I felt it was completely unnecessary. I don't like it when it disrupts the flow of the
lecture.

JOE: Yeah, she was looking at events I think of the period,
whereas Roger was looking at the thought. . . . And other
times you wonder if she has some kind of bias or some
kind of viewpoint that she's trying to enforce upon you
when she does something like that.

EMMA: I sometimes find it more helpful when she'll get up,
and she'll be [teaching] the second [class of the day], and
she'll say, "'This point, this point, this point, this point,'
and I respond 'this way.'" I find that a lot better than her
interrupting Roger's lecture or Thomas's lecture.

These complaints are a function, to some degree, of the time of the
semester. As one student put it, "We're swamped with papers and
exams, and you're asking us to talk about our opinions of the class.
Ask us over the summer when everything is done, and we'll be like,
'Ohh, I loved it so much.'" And yet, if the intensity of the complaints
would change outside the pressures of the semester, the focus of the
complaints would not. Students in a second, entirely separate focus
group, echoed the first group:

WILL: Olivia has been, from what I've seen, very into just
jumping in and doing a little mini-lecture inside some-
body else's class. I mean she is good about discussion, but
when it's another subject, I'd rather see her be a *part* of
the discussion than get up and teach a little bit.

ALAN: I liked how last semester the teachers would always get
involved, but they'd pose their own question, or they'd
say, "Well, I said this last time; do you think the same
kind of thing?" Not, "Here, let me teach you."

TYGRA: She has something from her own agenda that she wants
to throw in there, and she's not adding to the class that
we're in. And that's kind of hard. And yeah, sure, we'll
go back to it in her class—but that's Thomas's class. One

thing that really disturbed me in the beginning of the year was, I think Roger was talking, and she got up and starting writing on the board, and I was, like, "What are you doing!?" First of all, the chalk on the board was very distracting to what Roger was saying, and second of all I don't, I mean, I don't remember if it had any relevance to anything at all . . .

BETTY: Well, it doesn't bother me at all if she gets up and starts; I don't know, I just take what they're saying in little bits. Like I don't really worry about it being Roger's or being Olivia's or belonging. I don't think it's really important.

Olivia's efforts to teach for transfer—by coteaching with her fellow instructors (sitting next to each other, writing on the board as her co-instructor taught) and by talking in explicit ways about differences—violate students' expectations.

Part of the problem is that Olivia appears to be contravening a sense of propriety established during Interdisc I. As Alan explained it,

Last semester I thought it was a lot more respectful of their colleagues. It was like, "Here, let me ask you a question. Here's what I think, but how do you as the expert in this field take it?" . . . Last semester, and I don't want to seem too biased against this semester or anything, but there was a different type of interaction among the colleagues. Last semester had that happened, had the professor who was [leading the class] come back, the one who was sitting there would have said, "Hmm, that's interesting," and let them continue.

Alan clearly values the super-student ("Here, let me ask you a question") mode but resists the "interrupting" instructor engaging the "leading" instructor (whom Alan calls the "expert in this field") in sustained conversation.

Students draw on antecedent classroom genres to assess the appropriateness of interactions. Students are critical of this interaction because it's a mini-lecture, during which Olivia intrudes—apparently uninvited—into Roger's class. Their Interdisc I experiences had accustomed them to one instructor asking a question of another but not two instructors exploring differences. Students' resistance is reflected in the telling silence of their class notes; although students were clearly paying attention to this interaction, not one of the nine notebooks I read included any indication of this interaction (a fact discussed later in this chapter). The students are not sure if these extended interactions are relevant, and they're not sure if they're respectful, but they are certain that Olivia is violating the patterns of interactions familiar from the previous semester.

To underscore this point, Betty actively resists the critique of Olivia's participation. Betty was a transfer student who had not experienced Interdisc I and did not, therefore, bring to Interdisc II the same classroom genre expectations as her classmates.

Students' comfort with the super-student and resident-expert approaches to integration and students' resistance to the interdisciplinary-gadfly mode suggest another source of resistance. In her attempts to make visible the rhetorical dimension of disciplinary expertise, Olivia creates a space of conflict—a challenge not only to a sense of interpersonal propriety but also to the expectation that disciplinary expertise be respected. Alan was dismayed that a co-instructor would continue to challenge the "expert in th[e] field." Olivia's intent may have been to help students see conflict between epistemological positions, to help students denaturalize the "factual" expert knowledge that they accept as a given. But because the rhetorical domain was so new to students, all they could see was her challenge to authority.*

---

* Students' resistance to Olivia's mode of integration is also, I feel certain, grounded in gendered identities and expectations. Students' complaints that Olivia has "her own agenda" or "some kind of bias . . . that she's trying to enforce upon you" embody the resistance to feminist pedagogies described by Dale Bauer (1990). Olivia's extended, challenging interactions with her co-instructors violate not only the patterns of interaction established in Interdisc I, they violate expectations of women as collaborative conversational partners (Tannen 1994). Furthermore, Olivia identified herself as Jewish at least once during the semester; as Betty's experiences suggest, to be non-Catholic at this university was to be identified by many students as outside the mainstream. My analyses in this chapter suggest

Olivia strives to work politely with Roger and to minimize the interpersonal threat: she asks if they can have an argument (naming it as an activity that they can intentionally choose to engage in), and she makes sure that she's not cutting Roger off. Nevertheless, by naming their interaction as an "argument," Olivia may have unintentionally prompted students to interpret the exchange as an instance of interpersonal conflict, rather than an epistemological disagreement.

Olivia is attempting to create a new discursive space in which instructors engage in extended interactions, disagreeing with each other about epistemological issues. She's trying to carve out a new kind of role for teachers in class discussion and by implication new roles for students, too. By making visible the rhetorical domain of disciplinary expertise, she also challenges students' deeply (if tacitly) held beliefs about disciplinary authority, beliefs that are connected in the constellation of associations that attend the traditional genres of classroom interactions. To be an agent working against engrained interests and expectations is a risky business.

INSTRUCTORS AS HANDLERS: THE CHALLENGES OF ENCOURAGING TRANSFER

The primary task of a handler is to work behind the scenes to help students see and sell connections. In chapter 2, I suggest that one way for instructors to do so is to create more pliable discursive spaces in which students can perceive and respond to the relatively uncommon exigence of connecting knowledge, ways of knowing, identities, and goals associated with one context to another. The challenges facing instructors-as-handlers are significant and insufficiently explored in either the scholarship on transfer or interdisciplinary teaching.

---

that any teacher—man or woman, part of the dominant religious culture or not—would find that the interdisciplinary-gadfly mode challenges students' expectations for disciplinary expertise and potentially compromises her or his own authority. The authority Olivia ceded by highlighting the contingent nature of disciplinary knowledge was compounded by these other gendered challenges to her authority. A richer exploration of these dynamics is outside the scope of this chapter but an important area for future research.

A genred discursive space, however novel, is never entirely new. It always resonates with prior communicative exchanges, or what Kathleen Jamieson (1975) termed "antecedent genres." These antecedent genres, through which we perceive and construct novel situations, suggest a range of knowledge domains, ways of knowing, identity, and goals appropriate to the new situation. The appropriateness of those associations, however, can vary, and, as Jamieson notes, "the manacles of an inappropriate genre may be broken with varying degrees of difficulty" (414). This section explores the ways in which antecedent genres influence students' sense of what types of connections are invited or appropriate.

To do so, I focus on Roger's three history assignments: a medieval diary, two reaction papers, and a term paper. (The full text of the assignments can be found in the appendix.) One of these assignments encouraged a great many connections, while the others encouraged very few (see table 3.1). Students' responses to the assignments offer important insights into the types of genred discursive spaces that appear to invite transfer.

Table 3.1.
Presence of interdisciplinary connections in history papers (n = 35)

Paper	Number of papers with connections present	Number of papers with no connections present
Medieval diary (n = 9)	3	6
Reaction paper (n = 18)	14	4
Term paper (n = 8)	4	4

Together with a second rater, I read thirty-five history papers (four papers from each of nine focal students, with one term paper missing), working to identify connections to knowledge and ways of knowing associated with contexts other than history. We read and coded the papers individually, then talked until we came to consensus on every moment of connection that either of us had identified. In a later stage of analysis, I analyzed these papers again, drawing on my knowledge of student interviews to identify connections to identities and goals. As table 3.2 documents, the reaction papers contained the greatest number and variety of interdisciplinary connections: students made twelve knowledge connections, two ways-of-knowing connections, and one connection to identity and goals. Only four of the eighteen reaction papers showed no visible evidence of transfer of some sort; in contrast, six of the nine diaries and four of the eight term papers showed no visible evidence of transfer.

Table 3.2.
Number and type of connections in student papers for each assignment

Paper	Number of knowledge connections (content and proposition)	Number of ways-of-knowing connections	Number of identity and goals connections	Total number of connections
Medieval diary	2	—	2	4
Reaction paper	12	2	1	15
Term paper	—	—	4	4

The work that students did on these papers illustrates the ways in which genre—above and beyond the discipline or class structure or even professor him- or herself, which remained constant for all three assignments—can significantly influence the ways in which students make, and make visible, connections among previously distinct contexts.

Reaction Papers: A More Pliable Discursive Space

The Interdisc students were asked to write reaction papers to two book-length secondary historical texts. As Roger explained, "Reaction papers are simply that: your reactions, your personal reflection on what you have read, particularly as related to the course. [They] are not book reviews, strictly defined." Roger used these ungraded assignments as a springboard for class discussion. The striking number and variety of connections included in these reaction papers—fifteen connections, twelve of them knowledge connections—suggest the value of better understanding what in this assignment encouraged students to make so many connections visible.

Tygra's reaction to William Manchester's *World Lit Only by Fire* (1992) begins by reflecting on the author's preoccupations with "the corruption of the church and sexual promiscuity during this time period." Tygra then uses this knowledge as a framework for interpreting the Wife of Bath's prologue: "If what he asserts is true, then it drastically alters the Wife of Bath's personality and tale. It means she is not telling her tale in order to shock, but as a course of daily life." This is precisely the kind of connection that students might often choose to omit from their texts. Yet, here Tygra makes the connection explicit.

Why did the reaction paper assignment elicit such a different response than the term paper or medieval-diary assignments? The explanation is the associations students attach—or do not—to the genre of reaction paper. Most of the Interdisc students were able to describe a small taxonomy of academic papers (discussed in chapter 4). The reaction paper did not have a clear place in that taxonomy and therefore may have seemed a more pliable discursive space for many students, one with less strongly associated identities and goals and knowledge domains.

Students did seem to see it as separate from their usual academic writing: as Judy explained, "The reaction papers are totally different." One student, with a good-humored smile, described the reaction papers as "bullshit"—a term that suggests the degree to which this writing task did not fit into the taxonomy of genres that many students used to interpret most of their academic assignments. Furthermore, to the extent that students are aware of the processes of seeing connections and selling them to their evaluators, the fact that the reaction papers were ungraded likely made them a safer space to make connections visible.

Handlers who wish to help students see and articulate connections across previously unrelated contexts, then, might consider the possibility of not grading such assignments. Alternately, handlers might frame assignments within genres that do not have such strong disciplinary or academic associations. Such efforts will not inevitably meet with success, however, as the case of the medieval diary illustrates.

Medieval Diary: How Genre Can Encourage
Transfer but Frustrate Instructor Goals

The medieval diary was a deceptively simple assignment. The genre of diary served as an exigence for transfer, cuing students to connect knowledge, ways of knowing, identities, and goals they had associated with other contexts to the work they were doing in history. These acts of transfer, however, led some students to write papers that did not meet Roger's aims, and those students received lower grades. Handlers may find themselves in the position of having successfully invited transfer, only to discover that these acts of transfer distract students from the intended goals of the assignment. Unfortunately, such transfer can easily remain invisible to instructors, who simply see misinterpretations of the assignment.

Roger did work to be clear about his goals. The medieval-diary prompt, introduced on the assignment sheet as "Historical Creativity," asked students to "assume a specific medieval identity in terms of gender, age, social position, and occupation and write a diary entry for a single day." The goal of this assignment was to get students thinking about the material details of medieval life: the accumulation of minute detail, Roger explained in class, becomes significant for understanding everyday life. And diaries *have* often served as historical records of material conditions; the diary of Samuel Pepys, for instance, teaches readers a great deal about what people ate and drank, wore and did, as well as what Pepys thought and felt in seventeenth-century England.

However, framing the assignment as a diary taps into associations with diaries prevalent in late-twentieth-century America: as personal and private, as focused upon an individual's thoughts and feelings. A potential conflict, then, existed between the goals of the assignment (to focus on material detail) and the identities and goals often tacitly associated with the genre of diary (a self-absorbed author focused on feelings).

Students who received a high grade on this assignment understood the ways in which their prior experiences with the genre of
diary did *not* apply; those who received lower grades tended to write
diaries that included more personal reflection and less material documentation. Emma noted that she "wasn't sure if it was actually supposed to be like a diary. I guess with it being a creative assignment
you could pretty much do anything you want with it, but. . . . " Her
words trailed off, and she seemed to suspect that the assignment was
not "actually supposed to be like a diary." Similarly, Betty noted that
the medieval-diary assignment was *not* "totally creative . . . because
it was history and not like English." These authors engaged in what
Mary Jo Reiff and Anis Bawarshi (forthcoming) have termed "not
talk" as a way to understand their current task in relation to their
prior work in a related genre.

In contrast, Tygra relied heavily on the idea of a diary as a place
to explore feelings. Like Kelly—who was inspired by her reading
of Chaucer to write about the thoughts and feelings of a conflicted
nun (see chapter 2)—Tygra shifted the focus of her diary from the
material to the personal, composing a psychological portrait of a
hypocritical monk. Tygra's diary entry was, by her own account,
grounded in her own experiences (having gone on monastic retreat
with her mother) as well as her identity and goals as a person in a
self-described "tailspin" about religion and deeply concerned with
issues of religious hypocrisy. The constellation of tacit associations
surrounding the genre of diary encouraged Tygra to focus on personal reflection rather than material details. Tygra's act of transfer
may have imbued the assignment with additional meaning, but it
also resulted in a lower grade.

By framing the assignment as a diary, Roger in his capacity as
handler appears to have unwittingly set up a context in which the
genre of the assignment cued acts of transfer that were ultimately
counterproductive to the goal of the assignment. Instructors working
as handlers may, in some cases, be able to anticipate and avoid some
predictable conflicts among their goals and the associated knowledge
domains, ways of knowing, identities, and goals that constellate
around a genre. However, every student has an individual legacy

of schooling in which genres resonate with associations particular to the student's individual "chain of utterances"; given this reality, instructors working as handlers cannot anticipate all potential instances of "negative" (or, more accurately, "frustrated") transfer.

For example, Alan's work on the medieval diary appears to be influenced by an assignment he had encountered in Interdisc I; in that instance, each student had been asked to write a diary-like monologue that traced the inner thoughts and emotions of a character from Greek drama. The language that Alan used in a start-of-the-semester interview to describe his work on the Interdisc I character sketch ("Be as creative as you can. . . . I ended up doing a stream of consciousness essay") was repeated nearly verbatim weeks later as Alan described his work on the medieval diary: "He wants something creative. . . . I wrote a complete stream of consciousness."

Roger would not have likened the knowledge domain or goals of his diary assignment to the Interdisc I theater professor's character sketch; although in retrospect it is not difficult to connect the dots, Roger could not easily have anticipated this particular act of transfer. Alan, however, perceived a recurring exigence in both assignments: the necessity to write a creative, monologue-like account of a fictional-yet-historical person's experiences and feelings. Given this mismatch, Roger's comment on Alan's sketch of the emotions of a knight entering Jerusalem notes, unsurprisingly, that it was a "rather 'literary' piece for a knight."

To help students see and sell connections, handlers seek to find and to create more pliable genred discursive spaces—spaces that are not already saturated with prior associations. The success of some of these spaces, like the reaction papers, seems to be linked in part to the lack of constraints implied by a clearly determined academic genre—but perhaps more importantly by the lack of a grade. The challenge of some other spaces—even a diary, which does not have many clear academic associations—lies in the mismatch between the goals often associated with the genre and the goals of the instructor. The term-paper assignment, however, suggests ways in which even genres with long-standing academic associations can become more pliable.

History Term Paper: Defamiliarizing a Familiar Genre

Unlike the ungraded reaction papers and the nontraditional diary assignment, the term paper was a high-stakes assignment in an oft-encountered school genre. "The purpose of the history term paper," Roger's assignment explains, "is to 'write history' from original sources" found in a collection of primary texts (*The Old Regime and the French Revolution*) and other relevant sources. Roger explained in an interview that "it's probably closest to what historians do—finding a thesis in the original documents."

Only four visible connections were in these eight term papers: they all took the form of a prior interest that led students to choose their topics. Faced with the challenge of narrowing a workable topic from the task to write a "term paper on the French Revolution," Betty drew on her feminist commitments to write on women in the French Revolution. Similarly, Judy's self-declared "obsession" with John Adams and Thomas Jefferson led her to write on parallels between American and French forms of government.

The highly formal and heavily weighted nature of the assignment is directly related to the relative scarcity of visible connections in term papers. "There is room for resistance and transformation within genres," Bawarshi (2003) argues, "some genres more than others" (93). Although genres never entirely predetermine the actions of individuals, the associated knowledge, ways of knowing, identities, and goals constellating around genres are more firmly reified in some genres, more pliable in others. The term paper was a highly reified genre for most Interdisc students, one that left little room for acts of transfer that would distract from the goal of the paper—to demonstrate knowledge acquired through research.

Students approached the genre of term paper believing that they were to conduct research and report on it; they found little reason to make visible their other interests or knowledge—even if those interests might motivate their work in fundamental ways. For instance, Data acknowledged that he had selected his focus—the role of religion in the French Revolution—because of his growing religious convictions: "I think it's very clear that since I've had this . . . more intense interest in religion, that I would decide to do a religious paper." However, he never made his personal investment in this topic evident anywhere in the paper; this is unsurprising given Data's indication, during a separate interview, that he thought his personal interests and experiences should be kept apart from his academic work. When I asked what elements of his self and his personality he experienced most keenly in Interdisc, he answered, "I think in Interdisc the scholarly aspect of me comes forward because I think it's hard to, actually I think it's inappropriate to express, for example, your musical talent in a situation where no musical talent is required."

One lesson for handlers, then, is that some genres may prove a difficult space for making connections visible. Students' understandings of the identities and goals associated with school genres such as the term paper suggest to them the inappropriateness of bringing their own identities and goals to such work. These personal interests, identities, and goals may influence students' selection of topics and may in some cases further lead students to transfer knowledge, ways of knowing, identities, and goals that inform their work in substantial ways. Nevertheless, students may often choose to keep those connections invisible based on their understanding of the genred discursive space within which they operate.

The term papers offer handlers another lesson as well: even highly reified genres can be made more pliable. The only evidence of transfer in the term papers—connections to identities and goals—became evident when Roger encouraged students to alter their usual approach to the genre of term paper. He encouraged students to attach an "Author's Note" as a preface to their papers. In such a space, Roger instructed, students might explain their personal interests in the topic and justify the scope of the project. When I looked beyond my focal-student sample to the writings of all the students enrolled in the course, I found that six of the seventeen papers available to me did include an author's note in which the student made his or her personal interests and connections visible. Students explained their obsessions with Adams and Jefferson, their work as professional musicians, their love of art history born in a previous class. Although I would not describe some of these brief notes (often a sentence or a paragraph at most) as acts of transfer, they do begin to open up a space for student-as-agent and instructor-as-handler to recognize acts of transfer that may be influencing student work on these term papers. Genre expectations shape students' sense of the rhetorical options for selling their connections. Altering students' understanding of genre expectations can encourage them to make their connections visible (at least in limited ways).

The role of instructor-as-handler is an unwieldy one. Genres are always "handling" students—helping them to interpret, respond to, and even construct the discursive spaces within which transfer is possible—but who's "handling" the genres? The complex dynamics of working as an instructor-as-handler may be the least understood dimension of teaching for transfer, one worthy of future research.

INSTRUCTORS AS AUDIENCE: THE PROBLEM OF ASSESSMENT

Assessment poses particular challenges to instructors teaching for transfer. The institutional and epistemological structures of disciplines can make it difficult for instructors-as-audience to see and value the connections students make. And yet, if instructors aim to be teaching for transfer as handlers and agents, then they need to see those connections and evaluate them on their merits. Instructors in their capacity as handlers not only need to make space for students to see and sell connections, they need to create spaces where *instructors* in their capacity as *audience* can recognize and value connections. The Interdisc final exam offers an unusual but important example of teachers becoming their own handlers, opening up new options to students as agents and to themselves as audience.

An Unfamiliar Genre: The Collaborative, Oral Final Exam

Interdisc exists within a university structured by disciplinary divisions. The instructors wanted students to connect knowledge across disciplines, but the most familiar genres of assessment—papers and written exams—usually constitute and are constituted by disciplinary spaces that make it difficult to see and value such connections. The "manacles of inappropriate genre," as Jamieson notes, can be exceedingly difficult to break. The Interdisc professors and students thus required a new kind of discursive space. The Interdisc final was oral and collaborative. As the assignment sheet explains,

> A major premise of Interdisc II contends that significant shifts occur in many aspects of Western culture between the ninth and eighteenth centuries. This oral exam, which you will undertake in groups of three, asks you to analyze an aspect of this transition that you find particularly interesting by comparing two clusters of material that you select from different parts of the course.
>
> Each cluster should comprise one text from Theology; one text from Literature; and one text, development, or institution from History. You should select texts that, as a cluster, show significant similarities in light of your topic. You should select two clusters for the contrast they illustrate.

Students made a ten-minute presentation to the three professors, who then asked follow-up questions (at least one question per student from each instructor). Each professor also asked at least one question of each student—grounded in, but not limited to, texts or concepts studied in his or her discipline. Finally, each student was asked at least two "brief identification" questions—one or two sentences describing persons or concepts such as Oliver Cromwell, mercantilism, and the encomienda.

Was this a "new" genre for students and instructors? The oral and collaborative nature of this exam does make it remarkably uncommon in American approaches to higher education. Collaborative exams remain rare in the humanities, and oral exams are limited largely to foreign-language courses testing conversational proficiency, but the relatively unusual design of the final collaborative oral exam was *not* new to most of these students: fifteen of the eighteen Interdisc II students had encountered a similar exam in Interdisc I. Nevertheless, the final exam was an unusually pliable discursive space, a fact most visible in the creativity of students' presentations.

Each group began the exam with a presentation. Not one of the three groups I observed, however, relied on a traditional presentation format. In one group's "presentation," a student cramming for a final exam falls asleep and is visited in his dreams by Calvin, Blaise Pascal, Eve, the Wife of Bath, Galileo, and Queen Isabella of Spain. Another group tried a case in the "Court of Natural Law," with "tradition" and "modernity" vying for custody of the present day. The third group wrote a short two-act play—*Paradise Lost (Revisited)*—comprised of dialogue and epistles exchanged among Adam, Eve, and God. The students arrived in formal clothing (dress shirts and the occasional tie, skirts and pressed blouses) but also came with costumes (a judge's robe, a toga), props (an apple, a blanket and small Pooh bear, a large topiary), and in one case even musical accompaniment. At least four of the six groups actively resisted what Data called a "straight up thesis." In doing so, they both interpreted and constructed the exam as an unusual (and unusually pliable) discursive space.

It is easy to admire the students' creativity and to see how uncommon it is for them to take an oral, collaborative exam. What may ultimately be most important about this new genred discursive space, however, is the changes it makes possible for *instructors*. Throughout the semester, all the other means of assessment—the papers and the written midterm exams—focused on assessment of disciplinary knowledge through traditional means. The oral, collaborative exam structure, however, allowed the instructors to ask different kinds of questions, to see and to value connections students drew among the three disciplines.

The initial prompt for the final exam *required* students to draw connections across disciplines; the professors' questions, many formulated in response to that integrated argument, not surprisingly crossed disciplinary boundaries as well. Whereas only one of the professors' eight assignments and three midterm exams explicitly invited connections, nearly half of the questions asked during the final exam (twenty-five of fifty-three follow-up or short-answer questions posed during the three exams I recorded) required students to connect knowledge or ways of knowing from one discipline to another. On one occasion, for example, students were asked to read a passage from book 5 of *Paradise Lost* and identify theological allusions in each line. On another, students were asked to consider how the scientific revolution might have affected the ways in which authors from various disciplines theorized the morality of the Conquests. These exam questions were not unlike the connections made during class discussion—but they were *very* unlike the questions asked in prior papers and exams.

The pliable discursive space of the unusual exam format encouraged such questions. It would have been possible for the instructors to have collaboratively developed a paper assignment and evaluated it together—but they would have been struggling against established disciplinary expectations and patterns. Unlike the papers or midterms, this exam was designed to be given and graded collaboratively: instructors posed questions together and assessed the exam together, with all three instructors present in the same room together. By designing the exam in this way, the Interdisc professors opened up a different kind of space *for themselves*. They became their own handlers, creating a space in which they were able to see and to value connections that might otherwise have been rendered invisible or obscure. This exam structure opened up a space in which conversations among the professors about their shared goals and how well students met them were, though not inevitable, likely and appropriate.

Ultimately, the lesson for handlers is not that they need to create "new" genres to make connections visible. The Interdisc II exam wasn't new; it resonated both with the Interdisc I final exam and the in-class conversations students had participated in all semester long. But as a context for assessment, it was just different enough, just new enough, to overturn the usual expectations for final exams. This exam structure gathered all three professors and a group of three students together in a single room; in doing so, this "new enough" genre encouraged students and professors alike to inhabit and construct new identities and goals relative to traditional disciplinary boundaries and understandings of expertise.

CONCLUSION: TEACHING FOR TRANSFER AND THE GENRE OF THE STUDENT NOTEBOOK

By way of conclusion, I discuss one final classroom genre that persistently and nearly invisibly confounds instructor efforts to teach for transfer: student notes. My analyses are based on my readings of nine student notebooks. All nine students allowed me to copy their notebooks in their entirety, and one allowed me to copy both her original in-class "raw" notes and the "clean-up" version that she copied over each night.

Reading across the thousands of pages of these notebooks (most students had taken hundreds of pages of notes), I was struck by their consistency. Rather than keeping a single notebook in chronological order, every student kept separate notebooks for each of the three component disciplines. Their determination to keep these sections separate can be seen on those occasions when a class session was accidentally recorded in the wrong notebook: some students physically ripped out pages of history notes written in a literature notebook in order to tape them into the history notebook. Each student was determined to keep the notes for each discipline separate, even if it wasn't clear where to place the notes. For instance, the class session on Donne co-led by Olivia and Thomas appeared in some religious studies notebooks and some literature notebooks. In only one case did the notes give any indication that the session was cotaught by the two professors (Tygra, in the margins of her religious studies notebook, writes, "And Olivia too!").

Student notebooks are dominated by a series of bullet points recording facts. The rhetorical dimension of disciplinary knowledge, the contesting of and arguing over that knowledge—on the rare occasions that it became visible in class—remained invisible in the notebooks. The determination to record facts was so strong that it superseded even the most heated and memorable debates. These notebooks contain almost no sense of dialogue, of conflict, of people making arguments (not students, not teachers). With few exceptions, there is no attribution of who's saying what. Olivia and Roger's debate over the concept of the scientific revolution—one that students clearly remembered and had strong feelings about during the focus group—is entirely absent from seven of the nine notebooks I examined. In the remaining two notebooks, students recorded the following observations but made no mention of the debate:

> What actually happened determined by a few select elite. Not science unless the data is seen by one's own self (not someone else's data).

> Scientific revolution—what's the revolution
>   (a) philosophical impact

Any sense of debate is entirely erased. Similarly, one memorable history class period was consumed by a heated debate over capital punishment grounded in students' reading of Cesare Beccaria's *On Crimes and Punishments*; the only indication in any of these notebooks was Emma's note at the bottom of her page:

> woah . . . capital punishment discussion <yelling match>

The genre of note-taking discourages students from attending to contests over "fact," from recording the rhetorical domain. Although knowledge may be "forged in the heat" of debates of the sort occasionally made visible in the Interdisc classroom, student notebooks recorded only "cooled and hardened . . . truths" (Russell 1997, 528).

Henry's notebook was the only notebook to provide any sense of debate or competing ideas; occasionally, he would record the contributions of his classmates ("Agatha says . . . ," "Will claims . . ."), and rarer still he would provide a sense of disagreement ("The lone voice of Data resists"). His is the only notebook that gives voice to competing ideas in the classroom, but even Henry's notebooks contain only very brief phrases tucked into no more than a dozen of Henry's nearly four hundred pages of notes.

But why should this be? As Henry's note-taking proves, it is possible for students to keep notes of disagreements between individuals. However, these notebooks both respond to and create the situation they are responding to. Experience has taught students that they will be tested and held responsible for the facts and content of their courses; quite reasonably, then, that's what students write down and what they learn to *want* to write down.

When professor talk veers in unexpected directions—when, for instance, professors engage in debate—students are uncertain which "facts" to write down and often opt to write nothing. When students complain in interviews that what's going on in discussion "really does a number on my notes," they're not being flip. Taking good notes has been a key to success for many of these honors students. Most of them took hundreds of pages of notes during the semester.

Many of them copied their notes over each night. Some "cooked down" these notes into a dozen or fewer pages in order to prepare for exams. They're not being lazy when they say these cross-disciplinary explorations of the rhetorical domain of disciplinary knowledge "mess with" their notes: they're expressing genuine frustration that a significant contributor to their academic success is being threatened.

But if the genre of note-taking works against instructor-as-agent efforts to teach for transfer as an interdisciplinary gadfly, it also provides a potential site of intervention for the instructor-as-handler. With some encouragement and explicit instruction, within a context that makes clear the need and the benefits, students could learn to take different kinds of notes. If it was clear to students that the means of course assessment would value connections and/or a focus on ways of knowing, students could learn to record and reflect on debates in class, to focus on the rhetorical domain of the knowledge they are working to acquire in their notebooks. The potential for instructors-as-handlers is suggested by Henry's comments during an initial interview on his process of taking notes in Interdisc I:

> I always take into account . . . the interdisciplinary factor of it. When I'm reading in philosophy I've gotta think: okay, I'm gonna try to compare this to literature and history. When I rewrite my notes, I notice that I'm writing two things in two different subjects at the same time. And I note "Oh, look at the connection here."

Genres provide a powerful exigence for transfer, one that instructors teaching for transfer need to carefully consider and harness. This is true not only of connections among disciplines but also, as I argue in chapter 4, for instructor efforts to help students transfer writing-related knowledge.

4

"It's Really Hard for Me to Articulate, but I Know It's There": Transfer of Writing-Related Knowledge

[W]e must choose our genres carefully in order to serve our students best. What we assign today may appear in a new guise tomorrow. I suspect that the mechanism for writers selecting antecedent genres is not quite this straightforward. Writers may choose their antecedents for many reasons not necessarily related to the similarity of the situation, including such reasons as their comfort level with a particular genre or their resistance to a teacher or the genre the teacher promoted. We certainly need considerable research into how people make use of known genres when acquiring new genres.

—Amy Devitt, *Writing Genres*

AS AMY DEVITT CONSIDERS how best to teach first-year composition, she foregrounds the importance of antecedent genres for students' abilities to learn new genres and face novel demands. How exactly, Devitt wonders, do students use their prior genre knowledge to learn new genres?

The following exchange, recorded in one of my last interviews with Data, illuminates how one student wrestles with the relationships among different genres of disciplinary writing:

DATA: [English papers] don't seem to me intuitively the same thing as philosophy papers because it's English. And I guess I have such a mental distinction between English and philosophy that even though it may be the same sort of style in which we write, it's not the same thing.

RSN: And can you talk about that distinction just a little bit?
DATA: Well, for philosophy and theology we worked off of
someone else. Philosophy we worked off of Plato or Aristotle. Here [in theology] we're working off the six theolo-
gians we read. In English, we sort of work off of our-
selves. . . . I guess it's a difference of assimilation of the
text. I assimilated *Merchant of Venice* in a much different
fashion than I assimilated these guys because their style
was so different. And uhm, because I also had nothing
to cite but *Merchant of Venice*, so it was like . . . (*Data's
voice trails off.*) I don't know. It's really hard for me to
articulate but I know it's there. And that's part of it; what
I just explained is part of it, but it's something that would
require a lot of thought. I don't know.

To articulate the differences among his various papers, Data does not
turn to textual conventions like citation style or length or even kinds of
texts but instead tries to articulate different ways of engaging with and
making sense of texts. Not surprisingly, he struggles: "It's really hard
for me to articulate," Data sighs. "But," he insists, "I *know* it's there."

Data was a particularly reflective and articulate student, but he
was not unique. Many of these students worked in ways that were
sophisticated but ultimately limited as they tried to explain the
relationships among their various writing tasks. Students' genre
knowledge often focused on formal conventions but sometimes included richer understandings of larger rhetorical contexts and goals.
Students' genre knowledge was a dynamic cognitive construct, a
discursive space in flux, that helped them to recognize (however
tacitly) and articulate (however haltingly) connections among the
writing assigned in various contexts.

This genre knowledge made possible the relatively straightforward
act of transfer as application as well as more complicated, creative
engagements with novel contexts and purposes. Genre knowledge
in such cases enabled a process of reconstruction—a process that
can "repurpose" prior genre knowledge and even create new genre
knowledge (Reiff and Bawarshi, forthcoming).

Scholarship on transfer in the field of rhetoric and composition has understandably focused on first-year composition: what knowledge and abilities transfer out of and, less commonly, into FYC. Because the first-year students enrolled in the Interdisc sequence were not required to take the university's FYC course, the Interdisc classroom provides a window into a vastly different model of FYC, in which instructors of three linked disciplinary courses take responsibility for teaching writing. Examining transfer of writing-related knowledge within the team-taught learning community of the Interdisc II classroom allows me to ask, and answer, the following three questions: What do students know about genres? How do students make use of known genres when acquiring new genres? And, what can be learned about the transfer of writing-related knowledge by studying an instructional context not bound by the institutional limitations of FYC? These well-established limitations include trying to scaffold genre awareness in a classroom context not privy to the naturally occurring exigencies of disciplines, what Elizabeth Wardle (2009) calls the problem of "mutt genres."

HOW INTERDISC STUDENTS THINK
AND TALK ABOUT GENRE

Linda S. Bergmann and Janet Zepernick (2007) conducted focus groups with nearly forty undergraduates and concluded that

> these students seemed to connect with writing pedagogy only at a narrowly mechanical level and at a broad, moral level— taking away a series of behavioral "shoulds" that they remember and apparently accept, but don't necessarily follow. . . . [T]he astonishing blankness of the space between morality and the style sheet . . . is one of the most significant findings of our study. (137)

My study confirmed the two categories of knowledge Bergmann and Zepernick describe: moral imperatives and mechanical concerns. But students also described the importance of content knowledge for their writing and articulated a fourth kind of knowledge—knowledge of the formats of papers, that is to say, genre knowledge. (These categories are reminiscent of those presented by Christine M. Tardy [2009], who argues that "genre knowledge cannot exist separately from formal, process, rhetorical, or subject-matter knowledge; instead it is a confluence of these four dimensions" [20].)

My analysis of several hundreds of pages of interviews conducted with a smaller cohort of students at various points during the semester reveals what a focus group perhaps cannot: the middle was not "astonishing[ly] blank" but a protean space populated by talk of different types of papers that were associated with various content domains, mechanics, and writing strategies. Genre knowledge can be a complex and even contradictory cognitive space with the potential to mediate the three other categories of writing-related knowledge and thus a powerful resource for students attempting to transfer writing-related knowledge.

Content Knowledge

This category includes knowledge that is not obviously related to writing but that students presented as integral to their writing process—most often to their invention process. However, in their view, the role of content knowledge in the writing process is limited: these students appear to assume that content knowledge is already acquired before writing begins, not something constructed through the writing process. This view is (wrongly) affirmed by writing programs and "value-added" assessment policies that focus on writing as a portable "skill." The larger argument of this book challenges such an assumption: good writing is not a skill that can be extracted from the complex social contexts for writing and applied unproblematically. Rather, writing knowledge is actually a complex constellation of knowledges and abilities linked together by a writer's understanding of genre.

That said, students described content knowledge as something that made a particular assignment easy or a particular paper successful. Sometimes, this manifested as a general feeling of *confidence* in their understanding of what they'd read ("I understood Hume"). Other times, content knowledge was a *means of invention*: a sense of the *idia topoi* of the classroom ("I was just writing about 'lowering the ceiling,' which we've been talking about all semester"); of *background knowledge on a related topic* ("this reminds me of Ibsen"); or of more directly relevant *content knowledge*, often acquired in high school (Faustus as tragic hero).

Mechanics and Style

Students most often spoke of this type of writing-related knowledge as something they had mastered. This category clearly includes sentence-level, formal conventions such as grammar and spelling and also encompasses issues of style. The mechanics and style category also includes writing-related knowledge of citation styles and the formal conventions of incorporating and citing quotations from sources.

Writing Processes and Analytical Approaches

This category includes the kinds of moral imperatives that Bergmann and Zepernick identify; it also includes students' descriptions of their writing processes. In some cases, these were descriptions of their self-image as writers ("I'm such a crisis worker"; "I'm a big mark-up guy"; "I wait for the epiphany; I epiph"); in others, particular strategies (outlining, going to a book of quotations for ideas). This category also encompasses students' descriptions of their collaborative processes: discussing ideas with friends over lunch and the occasional self-sponsored peer-review session.

In addition to knowledge of their writing processes in general, students also described particular capacities they had developed as writers. Into this category, I place various "global" formal conventions (e.g., the ability to write an effective introduction, to compose a five-paragraph theme, to create "good flow" in a paper, to "use quotes well") as well as students' individualized strategies (e.g., "When I write a paper I write out my thesis and keep it on the bed next to me as I write in order to stay focused."). As with knowledge of mechanics and style, students often spoke of these abilities as skills they had mastered; they spoke of them in ways that implied these skills could and would transfer effortlessly from one context to another. However, that tacit assumption of portability was often wrong.

Genre Knowledge

The final category occupies a cognitive and discursive space between mechanics and writing processes. The students in my study talked a great deal about various *types* of writing—that is, about genre knowledge. Genres are not simply a collection of formal conventions but a means of rhetorical action, a discursive site through which formal conventions help individuals to both interpret and engage in the stabilized-for-now patterns of behavior and interaction and identity that constitute a disciplinary activity system. Not surprisingly, these first-year students did not have such a robust understanding of genre. For many students, genres were simply types of papers, with an emphasis on format and other formal conventions. However, students' genre knowledge was *sometimes* in flux. In situations that did not allow for a straightforward application of prior knowledge, genre knowledge was the place where students reconstructed the relationships between conventions and epistemologies, among mechanics, writing processes, and the aims of the various papers they labored to compose.

All eighteen students enrolled in Interdisc completed a survey that asked, among other questions, "What kinds of papers did you write in high school?" Five types of writing were mentioned by two or more students: research papers; analysis essays; creative writing; in-class, timed writing; and papers on math or science topics. The descriptions of these five "formats" of writing were remarkably consistent. The two most common genres, by a considerable margin, were the research paper and analysis essay.

I discuss the research and analysis genres in depth because as a researcher I was long tempted to dismiss these groupings as mere "school genres" (Beaufort 2007, 13) and the genre knowledge that informed them as naïve. How could such broad groupings reflect any nuanced understanding of the disciplinary activity systems that would inflect these overly general lumpings in significantly different ways? But a closer look at the history of students' engagement with assignments and reflections on genres challenged my assumptions and forced me to rethink the function and evolution of students' genre knowledge as they encounter new rhetorical situations.

The research paper was often also called the term paper; students generally described it as a major assignment and were eager to report on paper length (sometimes as short as six to eight pages, more often ten to twelve pages). The research/term paper was most often associated with the discipline of history but was also commonly connected to English classes. Less frequently, it was associated with science, math, and theology classes. An important component of the research paper is the gathering of information not readily available in class: Data, for instance, described a "very traditional term paper" as one "where you'd go get this material and have the works cited." Henry's view of the genre rested on the difference between "understanding" and "analysis": research papers require *understanding*, which is "a more scientific process of knowing how something works." *Analysis* (which he associated with literature classes) "is more of an opinion kind of thing."

Analysis essays were described as shorter (often three to four pages, sometimes as many as five to seven pages). If the defining element of the research paper is the gathering of source material, the central element of the analysis essay is the thesis. The "traditional literature paper," in Data's words, is, "This is my thesis, and here's how I back it up." The analysis essay was strongly associated with the discipline of English studies. For some students, however, this "thesis-driven" form of writing was less clearly associated with the English classroom and became their default mode for *all* academic writing. Emma, for instance, described her experience of listening to Olivia describe her expectations for the first literature paper:

> Olivia was talking about how to write the paper and someone asked, "Well, do you want a basic thesis or whatever?" and she said "No, no, no"—but then it seemed like that was pretty much what she described. At least what *I* had in mind as a general paper: starting with a thesis and then mapping out what you're going to say and then saying it.

The genre of analysis paper overlaps with what is often described as the five-paragraph theme: as one student put it, "A good four or five paragraph format where you can address one aspect of the topic and then another one and maybe a counterargument."

Students distinguish these two types of writing through varied and perhaps even contradictory means. Sometimes, the distinctions were grounded largely in formal conventions and content-domain associations (length of the paper, subject for which the paper was assigned). Other times, students understood the distinctions in terms of the goals of the assignment and the ways of knowing required in each—as in Henry's distinction between understanding and analysis. These shifting units of analysis reflect a basic reality of students' experience of transferring writing-related knowledge: students shift back and forth between formal conventions and broader epistemological constructions, between local knowledge and general strategies, between the conventional and the rhetorical. These two dimensions of writing expertise are, as Michael Carter (2007) claims, closely intertwined: "the specialized knowledge of a discipline . . . is not so special" and "the generalized knowledge of writing . . . is not so general" (410). For many students, the mental construct of a genre is the place where they are working out the complicated, protean relationship between formal conventions and the epistemological work of genres—and of disciplines.

One particularly important element of that evolving understanding is the associations students make between paper genres and disciplines. Research papers, for instance, may be associated most strongly with history—but students also associate them with English and math and theology and other disciplines. When students recognize that genres reach across disciplines, they are perhaps more likely to recognize that there are ways of doing and ways of knowing that exist above and beyond the content of a given discipline/subject (see Carter 2007). When students make these cross-disciplinary connections, a richer understanding of the rhetorical domains of genres and of disciplines becomes more likely (a claim also supported by Chris Thaiss and Terry Myers Zawacki's findings [2006, 106, 121]). Some readers might object that the "research paper," in its most adisciplinary and abstract form, is a fictitious genre; what writers encounter are always local instantiations of that overgeneralization. Nevertheless, the fiction of the "research paper" is a *usable* fiction, one that students carry from context to context and that potentially enables students to carve out distinctions between subjects and disciplines while tapping into their knowledge of qualities valued in academic writing more broadly.

To understand how genre knowledge helps students transfer writing-related knowledge across disciplinary boundaries, the next section examines how students use their knowledge of research papers and analysis essays. It looks at circumstances in which that knowledge transfer is unproblematic and those in which writers confront more challenging rhetorical situations (what I call "push assignments") that force them to creatively recontextualize their knowledge.

First, though, in order to better establish the context within which these students attempted to transfer their writing-related knowledge, I provide an extended portrait of instructor efforts to teach writing in the Interdisc classroom.

TEACHING (WITH) WRITING IN INTERDISC

This section describes eight writing-related moments in the Interdisc classroom. By showing the ways in which they build on and respond to one another, I develop three themes: (1) Students *do* transfer writing-related knowledge from one context to another, but that transfer is not always visible or valued; (2) even in an interdisciplinary learning community, it is difficult to sustain a shared pedagogical space for talking about writing; and (3) even in a disciplinary classroom, it is difficult to engage students in the kind of reflection on ways of knowing that can transform genres from collections of formal conventions into rhetorical resources. The presentation is chronological rather than thematic in order to highlight how the pedagogical spaces in which transfer occurs are constructed and constantly reconfigured.

Week 1, Thursday

During one of the relatively rare periods when he was the only instructor present, Roger announced that he would discuss a number of "logistical things" and that "it made more sense for me to do it when I'm alone rather than take up the other people's time." Among these logistics was an in-depth discussion of the history writing assignments. Roger's decision to not "take up the other people's time" with the "logistics" of his own papers illustrates one recurring theme: although teaching within a learning community provides instructors with more opportunities to develop a shared pedagogical space, actually engaging each other in that space can run counter to some basic impulses (e.g., don't waste colleagues' time).

Roger distributed copies of his assignments and explained his goals for each. He described his expectations for the term paper by explaining the difference between a "thesis" and a "topic."

> Step number one is to pick a topic. Notice step number one is not "I am going to prove that." That's not a topic, that's a thesis. A thesis is an argument. Topic is simply "I am going to write my paper about." So when you tell me your topic, it should be a phrase, not an argument. That comes later. The theory is that you're not sure what the argument is going to be until you've looked at the resources. You don't set out to prove something, you set out to see where the evidence leads you.

Roger concluded by explaining the goal of distinguishing thesis from topic: doing so can help keep students focused on "see[ing] where the evidence leads you"—a methodology he associated with the ways of knowing of historians.

This moment also introduces another theme: the difficulty of engaging students in ways of knowing and the rhetorical dimensions of disciplinary knowledge, rather than the formal conventions of genres. A larger disciplinary exigence motivated the term-paper assignment: how to engage with primary sources in order to understand past events. But in his effort to be explicit about his expectations, Roger boiled the rhetorical, disciplinary exigence down to the formal difference between a topic and a thesis. (This is a danger that, Aviva Freedman [1993] argues, dogs attempts to teach genre explicitly.) There was a disciplinary exigence, and there was an effort to convey that larger disciplinary exigence; nevertheless, as in chapter 3, instructors encounter a variety of obstacles (both internal and external) in their attempts to make ways of knowing visible to students.

Week 2, Tuesday

At the beginning of the next week, Olivia distributed an assignment asking students to "explain the difference" between a pair of critical comments on one of Chaucer's prologues and to "compar[e] the interpretation of Chaucer each position enables you to make." Although she was not present during Roger's earlier class, Olivia, too, initiated a conversation on the difference between thesis and topic. The students responded by transferring writing-related knowledge from one context to another; Judy echoed Roger's language almost exactly: "the topic is the broad overview of what you're doing, your thesis is your argument."

Olivia seemed to agree, initially distinguishing topic and thesis much as Roger did: "Yeah, your thesis is your argument. . . . A topic is what you're going to talk about. A thesis is what you personally have to say about it." However, Olivia articulated a goal considerably different from Roger's. A thesis, she said, "has to venture something. Peter Elbow, who's a writer about writing I like a lot, says it has to stick its neck out. If it doesn't stick its neck out, it's not a thesis."

Transferring their understanding of a thesis from Roger's class to Olivia's class, then, might lead students to misapprehend the goals and ways of knowing Olivia expected in their literature papers. Roger wanted students to start with a topic and work their way to a thesis; he left open the possibility that students might never articulate an explicit thesis: "At best," Roger said in his assignment, the paper "will argue to a conclusion, a thesis." During the last week of the semester, Roger even stated that the thesis might be "implicit in the paper" and not "expressly written in one place." For Olivia, having a clearly articulated and argumentative thesis in the paper was vital; a topic, which is "what you're going to talk about," cannot replace the thesis, which is "what you personally have to say" about that topic. Olivia's later assignment on *Doctor Faustus* also stressed the explicitly argumentative nature of the necessary thesis: "Please remember to . . . advance an argumentative thesis."

Like Roger, Olivia's assignment was motivated by disciplinary exigence: to advance an argument about a text using analysis of language as evidence. Yet, almost perversely, this very different exigence was also embodied in the formal convention of the thesis-as-distinct-from-topic. Olivia expected a thesis that would "stick its neck out" rather than a paper that would perhaps, at best, arrive at a thesis after "see[ing] where the evidence leads you." These different views of a thesis reflected significantly different ways of knowing. Many of those differences, however, were occluded by Roger's and Olivia's use of the same terms and their apparent agreement on the difference between topic and thesis. This unmarked contrast shows both how hard it is to create a pedagogical space to talk about writing and how hard it is to keep ways of knowing visible.

Week 2, Wednesday

As the week continued, all three Interdisc professors worked together to create a shared pedagogical space to discuss writing. For instance, during a class discussion of Richard Lanham's *Revising Prose*, the conversation unexpectedly turned to the question of whether student authors should incorporate questions into their prose. The conversation was prompted by one student's observation that Lanham's revisions resulted in questions, a revision Agatha resisted: "I hate beginning papers with . . . questions. I like starting with a solid statement." Olivia defended Lanham's revision and implied that nothing was wrong with using questions in a text:

> OLIVIA: My contention would be this: if for some reason that I don't fully understand, you have a problem with questions, you could probably use [Lanham's "paramedic method"] to come up with something that is assertive but far more pointed than this [original text].
> ROGER: For the record? I have a problem with questions, too, so don't do it for me.
> OLIVIA: But do it for me all you want. We'll get you confused. (*Laughter from class.*)

ROGER: There's a real moral there. You're not writing in the
abstract; you're writing for someone.

In this brief moment, the professors talk publicly about their writing
expectations and acknowledge their differences. Rather than shying
away, Roger capitalizes on their disagreement, using it as an opportunity to convey a "moral" to students—that they need to think
carefully about audience, rather than just relying on arhetorical rules.

Do these differences of opinion embody disciplinary divisions,
or are they simply personal idiosyncrasies? I'm inclined to think the
latter. Individual idiosyncrasy does play a role (perhaps, as Thaiss
[2001] argues, an underacknowledged role) in professor assessment
of student writing. However, the focus on the professor as individual
respondent with no mention of disciplinary differences may also
reinforce students' inclinations (see chapter 3; see also Thaiss and
Zawacki's [2006] three-stage model of the development of disciplinary writers [109–10]) to see the personal and the idiosyncratic rather
than any larger rhetorical or epistemological dimension.

Week 3, Monday

The difficulty of helping students to distinguish between personal
idiosyncrasy and conventions that reflect and create disciplinary
ways of knowing was thrown into relief during week 3. Olivia argued
against the limitations of the five-paragraph theme but in a way that
engaged more with conventions than disciplinary ways of knowing.
The exchange began when Judy asked, "Should we be following the
normal intro thesis support and conclusion thing?" Olivia explained
that papers under ten pages should not have traditional introductions
and conclusions, which are necessary only where a reader might
lose track of the argument. "Otherwise," she said, "that old five-
paragraph style is bad, bad, bad." Its primary fault is its tendency
to encourage repetition and knowledge dumps.

OLIVIA: In that first paragraph, somewhere in there has to be
your thesis . . . and a map of the terrain the paper's going

to cover. . . . . The last paragraph in an ideal world has some graceful closure, but that's a hard thing to pull off and . . . it is far better to end abruptly than to be redundant. In these short papers that you're writing for my part of the course just say what you have to say and stop. Err on the side of abruptness. Graceful closure is nice; it's just it's hard. Maggie?

MAGGIE: For this closure, you said it's the last paragraph. Does that mean it's going to be a closure of three to four, almost five sentences?

OLIVIA: No.

MAGGIE: It can just be two lines sticking out at the bottom?

OLIVIA: Yeah.

This was an important moment in the Interdisc classroom, one in which instructor and students struggled to communicate about the goals and format of the writing assignment in light of students' previous experiences. Olivia is asking students not to rely on the five-paragraph theme with its broad introductions and conclusions. But in the real time of impromptu classroom conversation, it is exceedingly difficult to talk about epistemological and rhetorical purposes and much easier to grasp onto formal convention—like the length of the concluding paragraph.

Particularly striking is the astonishment Maggie expresses in this exchange. She holds fast to her knowledge of conventions: a paragraph should be three to five sentences long. When told the conclusion can be shorter, Maggie expresses what sounds like distaste—"It can just be two lines sticking out at the bottom?"—as if her paper will be disfigured. Students who have little experience with the rhetorical dimension of disciplines and the epistemological dimension of writing cling to their knowledge of conventions. Making visible the rhetorical dimension of genres is a great challenge in teaching for transfer.

Week 5, Tuesday: Hour 1

Several weeks later, Olivia raised the matter of introductions again. This time, she worked more intentionally to explain the convention of short introductions and conclusions in light of the larger goals of the genre. "Here," she began, "is the way I wish I had explained it to start with."

> OLIVIA: What you are writing, in my part of the course, I think in Thomas's part of the course, and I think in most college writing, is the thesis-driven essay. So the question to ask yourself is, is this relevant to my thesis? . . . The paper is not about what you know about X. It's about your argument. So if you think about it that way, you will be clearer about what you do and what you don't need at the beginning and end of the paper. And I wish I had thought of saying it that way before.
>
> DATA: Do you mean for the entire writing of the paper we should consider what's relevant to the thesis? Or just the introduction?
>
> OLIVIA: Well, I don't think any of you were having a problem with doing it in the body of the paper. But some of you still had this introduction reflex where you think you need to say something sort of grand and general at the beginning and the end. And when I said to you, "No, just don't do it, just cross it out," it just didn't seem like as good a way of explaining it as saying, "If it's not helping you to prove your thesis, you don't need it."

Recognizing that her earlier attempt may have come across as an arhetorical rule (be abrupt in your conclusion—maybe just two sentences), Olivia attempts to reposition the convention as a way to achieve a larger rhetorical goal. The reason to break with the five-paragraph theme's "grand and general" introduction and conclusion is to avoid a knowledge dump: "This paper is not about what you know about X." Rather, the goal is to advance an argumentative thesis that sticks its neck out; staying away from general statements and asking "Is this relevant to my thesis?" are ways to achieve that goal. But despite Olivia's careful reframing of her earlier advice, students' inclinations to focus on conventions may make it difficult to put the genie back into the bottle.

Week 5, Tuesday: Hour 2

During the second hour of class, attention turned to Thomas's Aquinas assignment. Olivia's focus on an argumentative thesis offered a striking contrast to Thomas's first assignment, which was due within a week of the *Faustus* assignment and did not even contain the word *thesis*. The text of his assignment asked students to

> recreate the way in which, according to Aquinas, human beings achieve salvation. You will probably want to deal with issues like virtue and habit, grace, original sin, will, free choice, predestination, etc. . . . I want you to make a case for the reasonableness of Aquinas's theology on this issue. Be his defense lawyer. . . . Anticipate objections to the theory, and defend Aquinas against them. You should also describe what you feel to be the operative principles or problems around which Aquinas organizes his theology on this issue.

Students were puzzled by this assignment and asked for further explanation in class. One student remarked, "It seems to me that it [asks for] a regurgitation of Aquinas." In response, Thomas—perhaps picking up Olivia's language and claims from the hour before—used (for the first time) the word *thesis* to describe the paper for his class:

> When you analyze a writer, you're just not regurgitating. You're criticizing. It's a critical exercise—it has to be—because you are picking these things out, weighing them, arguing them. There's too much Aquinas for you to put into the paper, so you're going to have to choose, going to have to order and organize it into an argument. . . . So what you're going to do is present a Thomistic analysis of salvation. And it's very much like what Olivia . . . has been having you do [in in-class freewrites] when you analyze a text and you think like Aquinas. Well, I want you to *really* think like Aquinas. . . . What ties the system together? What's the most important thing about it? Why does it work or not work? Your thesis will probably come in that sort of a shape. The most important thing for Aquinas about salvation, [or] to understand Aquinas about salvation is

. . . He has a few major principles he's using. He's combining them. And then go through and say: "Well, given [Aquinas's] understanding of this, salvation works in the following ways." So it is a reconstruction of his argument.

As the assignment suggests and Thomas underscored, his overriding motive was to help students "think like Aquinas." By doing so, he explained, they would come to understand a worldview very different from their own and hone their analytical skills.

The Aquinas assignment required a thesis but one that advanced a type of argument unfamiliar to most students. Despite Thomas's claim that "it's very much like what Olivia . . . has been having you do when you analyze a text and you think like Aquinas," Thomas's expectations for a thesis were quite distinct. He modeled a thesis with madlib-type sentences: "The most important thing for Aquinas about salvation is _____," or "Given [Aquinas's] understanding of _____, salvation works in the following ways." Such a thesis is notable not for the degree to which it sticks its neck out but the degree to which it aptly identifies Aquinas's core assumptions and organizing principles.

Many students remained puzzled by Thomas's explanation—during an interview, Data called the paper a "critical, magical regurgitation . . . it's pseudocritical"—and they struggled to reconcile it with their understandings of the research paper and the analysis essay. For this reason, the Aquinas assignment was what I call a "push assignment"—pushing students to further develop and complicate their current understanding of genres.

Week 6, Thursday

The difficulty of creating a shared pedagogical space for teaching writing was further illustrated when Thomas invited students to ask questions about the Aquinas paper.

> HENRY: How do you feel about having questions in the text? Like actual questions?
> THOMAS: Uhm, that, that's fair—especially with Aquinas. Right? How does he proceed? Questions. So that's fair.
> HENRY: So we can put in, like, "How does this happen?"

Students *do* transfer writing-related knowledge from one context to another: Henry's question follows from Roger's and Olivia's brief discussion of the acceptability of questions during the second week of class. Henry remembers the conversation from four weeks earlier and—recalling that "you're always writing for someone"—asks Thomas's opinion.

Such acts of transfer, however, are not always visible to instructors. Although the Interdisc classes are linked, and there is some shared pedagogical space to talk about writing, Thomas was not present during Roger's and Olivia's discussion in week 2. Thomas's position here is like that of most instructors most of the time: he has no idea what connections motivate Henry's question. From the instructor's perspective, Henry's act of transfer can seem like a random, convention-obsessed question. Why, an instructor might rightfully wonder, would a student ask about whether he can include questions in this paper? This example illustrates the ways in which students' acts of transfer are sometimes not recognized or valued, as well as the difficulty of creating a sustained pedagogical space to connect the way teachers talk about writing—even in a team-taught learning community.

Week 11, Wednesday

The final vignette offers another example of how hard it can be to operate in the interdisciplinary-gadfly mode, to contextualize genre conventions within disciplinary epistemologies. This interaction was initiated by Olivia, who spontaneously responded to Roger's advice on developing a thesis:

> ROGER: Think in terms of the distinction now between a topic and a thesis. . . . A topic in a sense is a phrase: I am going to do a paper about blank. A thesis is a declarative sentence that is as particular as possible. (*Turns to Olivia.*) What were you going to say?
>
> OLIVIA: I was going to offer my definition of a thesis. . . . And if this doesn't work for history, this will be an interesting thing for us to find out. When you get to your thesis, you should be able to preface it with the words "I think that"

and then complete the sentence. And then when you're all done, to be more sophisticated erase "I think that." But if you can't say "I think that blah blah blah blah blah," it's not a thesis. Does that work for history?

ROGER: Ah, not too well. Because historians like to think that they're finding reality. So it's not just an opinion.

OLIVIA: Well, I don't think it has to do with opinion. What I think it has to do with is your personal analysis.

ROGER: Mm hmm. I think basically we're saying the same thing. I guess I feel more comfortable with it not prefaced by "I think that." That simply what would follow is a declarative sentence in itself.

OLIVIA: (*Turning to the class.*) I want to make sure you guys are clear that you would never hand this in to anyone with the "I think that" still there. But some of you might want to think maybe in other disciplines about that. And I would still say that if you think about it analytically instead of subjectively, that might help with history. Right? Because you can't say, "I think that the French Revolution." But you can say, "I think that a change in sexual mores produced the French Revolution."

ROGER: I see. Actually it comes out the same because it has to be a declarative sentence.

OLIVIA: Right. Okay.

Olivia does open up the possibility that there will be differences in their expectations: "if this doesn't work for history, this will be an interesting thing for us to find out." Roger does initially resist what he sees as a difference in ways of knowing manifest in the textual convention Olivia is proposing: using "I think that" wouldn't work "because historians like to think that they're finding reality."

Roger and Olivia did read texts differently—a fact made evident in a group interview with all three professors. Thomas explained, as Roger nodded, that for the two of them "texts are just instruments"—whereas in literature "the texts are a source of endless aesthetic literary pleasure: the more interpretations you get, the better."

Olivia, however, disagreed: "I'm interested to hear you talk about the multiplication of interpretations because . . . I don't feel that is actually the point of what I'm doing." She explained that she was less interested in "endless literary pleasure" than in helping students to develop "interpretive suppleness" by "seeing how to put together an argument more than one way." To do so presumes that texts are more than just transparent instruments.

And yet, despite these different ways of reading and knowing, once Roger and Olivia find they agree that the phrase "I think that" should not be in the text of the thesis, they cease to pursue the possibility of more significant differences. As chapter 3 argues, the clear tendency for both students and instructors is to stress similarities among disciplines and overlook the rhetorical domains of disciplinary knowledge.

The language that seemed most readily available to the Interdisc instructors—the language of thesis and argument—functions as what Janet Giltrow (2002) calls a *metagenre*. Metagenres "provide shared background knowledge and guidance in how to produce and negotiate genres within systems and sets of genres" (Bawarshi and Reiff 2010, 94). Yet, the metagenre of *thesis* did not adequately equip students (or teachers) to distinguish between the multiple institutional laminations that Thaiss and Zawacki (2006) argue inflect instructors' expectations for academic writing: disciplinary and subdisciplinary expectations, institutional and personal idiosyncrasies, and broadly shared standards of academic writing (60). Instead, the language of *thesis* erased nearly all those distinctions, leaving students-as-agents in the perilous position exemplified by Tygra's experience writing the *Faustus* paper (see chapter 2).

This account illustrates the limitations of the language of *thesis* as a metagenre crossing disciplinary boundaries. But it also illustrates the important role that the dynamic cognitive construct of genre plays as students attempt to transfer writing-related knowledge from one instructional context to another. Genre is a powerful resource for students as they encounter rhetorical situations that seem familiar and as they encounter push assignments that alter and expand their understandings of writing and sometimes of the disciplines themselves.

TRANSFER AS APPLICATION

Transfer as application involves the relatively simple connection of knowledge, ways of knowing, identity, and goals associated with one context to another; it is akin to what David N. Perkins and Gavriel Salomon described as "low-road transfer" in which "the new context almost automatically activates the patterns of behavior that suit the old one" (1988, 25). An example of transfer as application can be found within the literature papers.

Despite Olivia's efforts to distinguish her assignments from "the normal intro thesis support and conclusion thing," many students described the literature assignments as conforming to their prior expectations and experiences. Judy was an English and honors major, with a minor in education. In her estimation, the literature assignment on *Faustus* was

> . . . a straightforward literary high school analysis assignment.
> . . . It was difficult because I had problems figuring out what my thesis was going to be and what the low characters were all about . . . but once I had [my thesis], it wasn't terribly difficult.

Judy's prior genre knowledge provided her with a means of interpreting the task and composing a text that seemed fully adequate for the new context; in this case of transfer as application, there was no need for transfer as reconstruction.

TRANSFER AS RECONSTRUCTION
AND "PUSH ASSIGNMENTS"

The Aquinas assignment, however, pushed students to engage in a very different process of transfer. Henry initially interpreted the assignment as a research paper, but writing the paper altered his understanding of the assignment and of genres. Will, who wrote his literature papers easily, labored over the Aquinas paper and was puzzled by his success. Both cases illuminate how genre knowledge serves as a resource for students transferring writing-related knowledge.

Henry: "Not Talk" and Genre Knowledge Development

Henry was the self-described "court jester" of Interdisc and a math major with plans to attend medical school. Henry described himself as "not a humanities guy" and "not much of a writer." Through his engagement with a push assignment, Henry's genre knowledge was challenged and his sense of antecedent genres perhaps expanded. As he began the Aquinas paper, Henry was what Mary Jo Reiff and Anis Bawarshi (forthcoming) call a "boundary guarder," confident that the assignment was adequately explained by his existing knowledge and prior experiences. Through working on the Aquinas assignment, Henry became more of a "boundary crosser," understanding and using his antecedent genre knowledge in novel ways.

For Henry, research papers require a more "scientific" process of "understanding" facts, while analysis papers require fewer facts and more arguments to forward an opinion. Before writing the Aquinas paper, Henry explained his interpretation of the task by comparing it to the second literature paper (on Christopher Marlowe's *Doctor Faustus*), due at roughly the same time:

> This [Aquinas paper] is not an argumentative paper. I'm not arguing [Aquinas's] position. I'm pretty much explaining his position. That's, I think, the key difference. While on the other [*Faustus*] paper, I'm gonna argue a position about the social standing of those scenes.

In order to interpret the assignment, Henry compares not just formal features (like length and subject matter) but deeper goals.

Henry's initial dichotomy between the genres of research and analysis was so well established that he understood them as totally different mindsets that needed to be kept separate. Anticipating a weekend of writing papers for religious studies and literature, Henry described his ideal writing process:

> I'd like to block out a whole half a day for the assignment. I mean not go back and forth between the two. Just focus primarily on one, and give myself a BIG break in between—whether it's literally a night or a three-hour break in which I do nothing. Because . . . [i]t's two different kinds of thinking. When I read Aquinas, it's just a different kind of reading; I'm reading like a textbook almost. While [*Doctor Faustus*] I'm reading more for interpretation, which for me is just two different kinds of mindsets.

Before he started the assignment, Henry thought of it in terms of the contrast between literature and theology. He read Aquinas's *Summa Theologica* like a textbook, looking for the facts necessary for his research-type paper. He read *Doctor Faustus* for interpretation, trying to develop an opinion to argue. However, the actual experience of writing the paper led him to articulate his understanding differently, in a way that breaks down the research-analysis dichotomy and potentially articulates new genres.

Henry didn't entirely abandon the research-analysis distinction, but during a post-paper interview, Henry positioned the Aquinas paper quite differently in relation to his preexisting genre knowledge. The knowledge Henry identified as most important was not his experience with other research papers but with his Interdisc I philosophy class.

In an initial interview, Henry had described the previous semester's philosophy papers as challenging, his tone of voice suggesting amused bewilderment: "And then philosophy? Ooohh boy! Philosophy. . . . Whenever I handed in a paper . . . I was like 'You know what? I didn't know what I was writing!'" While writing the Aquinas paper, however, the experience of writing the philosophy papers apparently provided clarity and insight.

RSN: Could you or would you have written this religion paper the same way earlier in the semester?

HENRY: Uhm, yeah, because it was similar to my philosophy last [semester]: the taking of concepts and showing that you understand it. Not before first semester, but before second semester.

RSN: Yeah? And could you just briefly describe what it was that you learned in the first semester that would have enabled you to do it differently? Or forced you to do it differently?

HENRY: Well, let me think, because you know it was last semester. (*Pause.*) In a critical analysis, I think it's just, "What does it mean, what is its meaning?" Aquinas does write in black and white—so now I just have to say, "Well, what's his project?" There you go. That's exactly it. Big thing is what the guy's project is. What's his intention? Ok, and I'd never read anything like that before my previous

philosophy [class]. And [the Interdisc I philosophy profes-
sor] kept saying, "Well, what's Aristotle's project in this?"
So I, I even remember writing "Aquinas's project is." I'm
almost positive I wrote that. Just because, well, this is
what he wants to do. So instead of . . . this is a bunch
of facts about [salvation], now I just collect them in that
[focus on Aquinas's project].

The major challenge of the Aquinas push assignment was finding the
balance between summarizing facts and advancing an opinion-based
argument. For Henry, critical analysis involves opinion: "What's its
meaning?" But Aquinas was too "black and white" to fit into that
genre. However, based on Thomas's in-class discussion of the paper,
Henry knew he was supposed to have an argument.

Ultimately, Henry found that his dichotomy between research
papers that report on facts and analysis essays that valorize opinion
could not fully account for the Thomistic analysis of salvation required in the Aquinas paper. Rather, it was his prior experiences in
philosophy class that finally enabled Henry to come to terms with
the Aquinas assignment. Instead of just reporting on facts—as he
predicted he would before he actually wrote the paper—or writing
a critical analysis of "What does it mean?" Henry made adjustments
to his usual approach to the research essay. Inspired by his prior
work in philosophy, Henry asked not, "What does it mean?" but
"What is his project?" Henry "collected" those facts around the idea
of Aquinas's project. Henry was able to compose his paper through
a process of comparing and combining the goals he associated with
different types of papers.

Henry's Aquinas paper became a sort of bricolage, combining
elements of research and analysis papers. Henry could have limited
himself to his most clearly established categories of genre knowledge
and been paralyzed when the Aquinas assignment did not fit neatly
into either. He was not. He might have proceeded blindly, insist-
ing on using an ill-suited antecedent genre. He did not. Instead,
Henry drew connections to a prior encounter with a previous push
assignment—the philosophy papers of Interdisc I—to imagine a

"new" antecedent genre. As Henry wrote the Aquinas paper, he acted as bricoleur, altering the genre of research paper by creatively recontextualizing strategies he associated with philosophy papers ("What's this guy's project?"). Henry succeeds by making connections and drawing comparisons and by engaging in what Reiff and Bawarshi (forthcoming) term *not talk*. It is his willingness to treat genre knowledge as more than a coterie of conventions, his willingness to see the links between formal conventions and larger rhetorical purposes, that helps Henry to connect writing-related knowledge from his earlier philosophy class to his current Aquinas paper.

Through this process, Henry may also be bringing to conscious knowledge a new genre—or new to him at least. By drawing on prior philosophy papers to make sense of his current theology paper, Henry begins to see a pattern across disciplinary contexts. He begins to see shared goals across disciplinary boundaries, and he draws on this prior knowledge to face his current task. Transfer, in this case, is a process of reconstruction: Henry's understanding of the assignment is reconstructed from one of a factual, scientific research paper to a more complex hybrid focused on "What's this guy's project?"

Will: Genre Knowledge and Meta-Awareness

Will, a first-year student with a double major in religious studies and philosophy, earned high grades on all his papers; all three professors identified him as one of the most successful students in the class. Will's understanding of the genres of research papers and analysis essays helped him to interpret and compose his papers, and his encounter with the Aquinas push assignment illustrates how a student's genre knowledge can enable transfer of writing-related knowledge without fully conscious awareness.

Analysis of Will's texts indicates that he made subtle but important adjustments to his essays in each discipline, decisions that resulted in high grades. But Will was vexed by the process of moving among the various disciplinary expectations—in part because he hadn't developed a fully conscious understanding of the rhetorical dimensions of these essays.

According to Will, the literature paper on *Doctor Faustus* was very clearly an analysis essay and the history term paper was a traditional research paper. Because these two assignments fell easily into Will's well-established genres, he was able to apply his prior genre knowledge using antecedent genres. But the Aquinas paper did not fall neatly into either of Will's two genres, and as a result, he struggled to develop a thesis. When asked about the Aquinas paper, Will began by describing the unique writing process it required.

> It was really hard to jump into. . . . I wrote this one actually a little differently than I write a lot of papers. . . . Usually when I've had to do a paper of that length, it was more like a research kind of thing where I'd been working on it and studying it with the intent of writing the paper. . . . But this time it was really just like the [analysis] essays I write usually but a lot longer and covering a lot more material.

Although he finally had decided it was an analysis paper, Will spent almost no time working on the thesis statement and introductory paragraph: "the intro and conclusion were also very hard. I did those in about five minutes combined, just because I really didn't know what to say in them." For Will, articulating an argumentative thesis was secondary to showing mastery of the component parts of Aquinas's model of salvation.

Differences were evident in the text itself as well. Whereas the thesis guiding Will's *Faustus* paper made a clear argument about the relationship between the low scenes and the main plot of *Faustus*— "This subplot of *Doctor Faustus* parallels Faustus' own downfall, and his actions toward them mirror the actions taken against him"—the thesis statement of his Aquinas paper surveyed the component parts of Aquinas's model of salvation but did not "stick its neck out." Will identified an important tension in Aquinas's work in the penultimate sentence of his introduction ("This comprehensive discussion ultimately leads to a model of salvation that acknowledges the omnipotence and supremacy of God as well as the importance of humans' contributions to their own futures") and overviewed the organization of the paper in the final sentence. Will described this thesis as more summary than argument.

When Will encountered an assignment that did not fit into his established genre categories, he was forced to reconstruct the writing-related knowledge he had acquired in other classes and contexts. He had to creatively recontextualize this knowledge, abstracting and repurposing strategies associated with one genre to write in what felt like another genre. Will described the bricolage of his Aquinas paper: "This time it was really just like the [analysis] essays I write usually but a lot longer and covering a lot more material." Will recombined the formal conventions of length and scope of research papers with the more argumentative focus of analysis essays. The result was an A paper but a puzzled student.

Will doubted whether this was an appropriate way to write a thesis and even described his thesis as "a cop-out," as merely "a rehashing or a reformulation" that wasn't "arguing" any one particular point. It wasn't, in Will's evaluation, particularly "insightful." Whereas analysis papers usually demand something more than "regurgitation," Will said the Aquinas paper was a regurgitation "more than he wanted to let on" since it was only "the structuring, kind of putting it in our own logical flow, that was original."

Will had intuited the differences in the goals of the various disciplines he was being asked to negotiate. But that knowledge never manifested as a fully conscious awareness. Will wrote successful papers but remained puzzled by his success. Yet, there was transfer. Will used strategies that had served him well in the past, though he used them in different ways and for different purposes than he was accustomed.

Will's example illuminates how a student can succeed in a context that requires transfer as reconstruction—even without the ability to articulate the new genre within which he is working. Will's genre knowledge—particularly his understanding of the rhetorical goals and dimensions of this paper—appears to be more tacit than conscious. That tacit awareness is constituted in part (though not fully explained) by the creative recontextualization, the not talk and repurposing and bricolage, made possible through Will's understanding of the genres of research paper and analysis essay.

CONCLUSIONS

This chapter continues to advance the argument made in earlier chapters: that students do, in fact, transfer writing-related knowledge from one context to another but that these instances of transfer are often not recognized (e.g., Henry's inquiry about using questions in a paper) or valued (e.g., the distinction between topic and thesis established in history class was not entirely suitable for literature class). To make this argument is *not* to suggest that students would not benefit from further efforts to encourage them to connect knowledge from one context to another: the students in my study are honors students, who may make more connections than the average student; the process of participating in my research may have provided them with more opportunities to articulate connections; and no evidence suggests that students can receive too many cues for transfer. To make this argument does, however, underline that the institutional structures of colleges and universities grant instructors the power to recognize and value connections while making it difficult for them to actually do so.

This chapter also introduces the particular challenges facing instructors attempting to work as agents and handlers teaching for the transfer of writing-related knowledge. The eight vignettes at the heart of this chapter show how even in an integrated and interconnected learning community—one in which instructors plan syllabi together and attend each other's classes—it is remarkably difficult to build and maintain a pedagogical space to discuss the role of writing in the disciplines. One challenge is logistical: how can one instructor know everything another instructor has told students? But the more pernicious challenge may be uncovering the rhetorical domains of the disciplines and helping students to see connections between the formal conventions and rhetorical dimensions of genres.

This last problem—one of genres devolving into collections of formal conventions, disconnected from disciplinary exigencies—is one that Wardle (2009) termed, in the context of FYC, the problem of "mutt genres." The examples of Will and Henry affirm Wardle's claim that instructors should expect little ability to transfer writing-related knowledge when students understand genres as a collection of formal conventions with no connections to larger goals or disciplinary activities. What's more, by looking at the challenges of writing and learning within the institutional context of Interdisc, this study also demonstrates that the problem of mutt genres may be more pervasive than FYC-based studies of transfer have suggested.

Even within disciplinary classrooms, it remains difficult to engage students in the full work of the disciplines. This is due partly to the fact that the activity system of the general education classroom is divorced from the activity system of the discipline (Russell 1997). It is also exceedingly difficult (as chapter 3 argues) to make the rhetorical domain of disciplinary expertise visible to students who aren't aware that such domains exist, who see only content knowledge and formal conventions and personal idiosyncrasies.

The examples presented here suggest that, at least in regard to writing, students may not necessarily benefit from the explicit teaching of genre offered by instructors-as-agents. Olivia's initial efforts to teach the genre of literary analysis by challenging students' attachment to the five-paragraph theme ended up focused on formal conventions; her later attempts to make clearer the links to the rhetorical purposes of the writing went largely unheeded by students who continued to focus on formal conventions. This observation echoes Freedman's (1993) argument against explicit genre instruction: explicit instruction that specifies "the (formal) features of the genres and/or . . . [the] underlying rules" (224) may be unnecessary and perhaps even counterproductive as it may short-circuit fuller immersion into the rhetorical context and exigencies that make genres necessary and meaningful.

Yet, based on my case studies, I would not abandon genre pedagogy entirely. To teach genre explicitly is to act as an agent—seeing the connections for and selling them to students. The research presented in this chapter suggests the importance of instructors acting instead as handlers, finding ways for students to become agents and wrestle with the rhetorical domain of disciplinary knowledge in their writing. Instructors-as-handlers can create push assignments that challenge students' preexisting conceptions of genre and encourage them to probe the relationships between formal conventions and disciplinary purposes (Devitt 2009). Under such circumstances, encountering such prompts, students can actively work as agents by creatively recontextualizing strategies and goals and conventions from the genres they already know.

Learning communities open new possibilities for handlers committed to genre pedagogy, including a shared pedagogical space in which instructors can discuss their goals and expectations for writing. That shared pedagogical space, as this chapter demonstrates, is difficult to build and maintain. But within that shared pedagogical space, instructors-as-handlers might encourage students to grapple with the various assignments and expectations not only by considering their connections to students' antecedent genre knowledge but also by exploring the similarities and differences among the assignments they are working on within the learning community.

This chapter began with the question of how students make use of known genres to learn new genres. By looking at student writing and students' talk about their writing, I conclude that students extend their genre knowledge and transfer writing-related knowledge by acting as bricoleurs. Students sometimes work not fully consciously, making comparisons among the formal conventions and sometimes the rhetorical dimensions of their various papers. Prompted by such comparisons, students may abstract strategies and repurpose them, becoming bricoleurs. Being a bricoleur—comparing and combining and making connections, abstracting and repurposing strategies—is the work that students need to do as agents of integration.

The process of encountering push assignments and engaging in such bricolage will not inevitably lead students to a full awareness of the rhetorical domain of disciplinary writing and knowledge. But instructors can support and scaffold this expansion and transformation of genre knowledge by giving students opportunities and reasons to discuss their understandings of antecedent genres. Within the shared pedagogical space of a learning community, such conversations might unfold differently, perhaps resonate more richly, than they would in a single, traditional classroom.

5

Implications

> When I am at my best as a learner, I am like Super Glue. . . . Super
> Glue can form bonds between all kinds of objects; it is versatile.
> At my best, I can draw connections between lessons I have learned
> across different areas of knowledge, forming unexpected links.
> There is another similarity between Super Glue and my learning
> ability. Just as I am completely unable to explain how Super Glue
> works, I am also incapable of explaining what enables me to learn
> well when I am at my most effective. I just know that it works.
> —Justin, a political science and economics major

JUSTIN IS NOT AN INTERDISC STUDENT. He was enrolled in my recent
advanced composition class—a stand-alone course taught at a different university. Nevertheless, Justin's Super Glue metaphor illustrates
the degree to which students outside the Interdisc classroom share
my focal students' enthusiasm for "forming unexpected links" as well
as their inability to explain what exactly makes those links possible.
Justin's zeal parallels that of the Interdisc students and suggests the
need to consider the ramifications of the theories developed from this
single case study for contexts outside of Interdisc. This final chapter
explores the implications of this study for first-year composition and
for writing centers, as well as directions for future research.

IMPLICATIONS FOR FIRST-YEAR COMPOSITION

A central preoccupation of transfer scholarship in rhetoric and composition has been the relationship between first-year composition,
genre, and disciplinarity—a relationship that this study of Interdisc
is well positioned to interrogate. FYC instructors have historically

taught the modes of discourse or valorized certain genres as preparing students for future success. The problem with this approach, as Elizabeth Wardle (2009) notes, is that these genres tend to operate not as genuine "boundary practices" preparing individuals to participate in communities of practice beyond FYC but as "mutt genres." Mutt genres echo the forms of naturally occurring genres—but because this writing does not respond to a genuinely (re)occurring exigence, students learning mutt genres focus on formal features rather than the rhetorical work accomplished by the genre. Without experiencing the exigencies that give form and meaning to genres, students will not develop writing knowledge that can effectively transfer to other contexts.

One radical response to this critique has been the call to abolish FYC, replacing it with a series of writing-intensive courses. A more moderate approach to FYC has stressed teaching critical genre *awareness*, an approach whose "primary task" is "to keep form and context intertwined" (Devitt 2004, 198). A third response to the problem of mutt genres has been to reconfigure FYC as a disciplinary course about writing, grounded in the study of genre and invention particularly (Bawarshi 2003, 168–69) or the discipline of rhetoric and composition more broadly (Downs and Wardle 2007; Wardle 2009).

This study suggests a different response to genre-theory critiques of FYC, one that locates the problem of writing-related knowledge transfer within the larger challenge of becoming an agent of integration. In particular, this research foregrounds the value of helping students see the rhetorical domain of disciplines, because disciplinary divisions (both institutional and epistemological) pose a significant obstacle to integration. I begin by outlining a relatively ambitious revision of FYC modeled on the Interdisc classroom and then explore the somewhat more modest implications of this research for traditional FYC courses.

First-Year Writing Instruction in an
Interdisciplinary Learning Community

One major finding of this study is the challenge and value of contextualizing FYC instruction within disciplinary inquiries. To facilitate transfer of writing-related knowledge, FYC can help students see the connection between formal conventions of written genres and disciplinary epistemologies by immersing students in the disciplines. A first-year writing course designed to help students become successful agents of integration must take seriously the imperative to create an institutional context that pulls back the curtain on the formation of disciplinary expertise. Although metacognitive awareness is not always necessary for successful transfer of writing-related knowledge, an ability to recognize the rhetorical dimensions of disciplinary knowledge is relatively rare for first-year students and may help students transfer writing-related knowledge.

The paradigm of locating writing instruction within "writing-intensive" disciplinary classes is well established, but a model for writing instruction located within an interdisciplinary learning community is not. Such a model might be called an *interdisciplinary learning community (LC) model* of first-year composition. This model differs from the more common linked-courses model (in which a section of FYC is linked to another course—usually an introductory-level, general education course) by eliminating the dedicated FYC course and embedding responsibility for writing instruction within a learning community taught by non-FYC instructors.

My study was not comparative; I do not make claims for the merits of this model compared to the traditional stand-alone or linked-courses models. (Some research presents the linked-courses model as a rewarding approach that breathes new life into FYC [Zawacki and Williams 2001; Dinitz et al. 1997]. Other research argues that the problems facing traditional FYC courses are continued or even exacerbated [Wardle 2004, 2009] by the link.) However, my research suggests—and Chris Thaiss and Terry Myers Zawacki's (2006) research affirms—that the comparative work that an interdisciplinary LC enables provides a significant advantage for students developing an understanding of disciplines rather than subjects.

The interdisciplinary LC model might take a variety of forms in different institutional contexts, but curricula based on the interdisciplinary LC model of first-year writing instruction would meet four basic criteria:

✓ Two or more courses (none of which is a dedicated FYC course) linked into a learning community; a cohort of students takes these courses together

✓ Assignments that engage students in the intellectual work of the component disciplines

✓ Regular contact among the instructors inside and outside of class

✓ Structured opportunities for students to reflect on the similarities and differences between the types of writing-related knowledge valued in each discipline

The interdisciplinary LC model is patterned after a course that, without doubt, exists in a context of tremendous institutional privilege. The instructors are given a course release to support their participation in colleagues' classes; they are tenure-track or tenured professors who are able to build long-term relationships over many years. A small number of students is recruited by the honors director who serves as their academic adviser; he or she arranges their schedules around their participation in the LC.

To what degree can such a model be replicated at other institutions? And to what degree can it be scaled up to serve more than twenty students each year? The answers to these questions of replicability and scale hinge on three other questions: what kinds of students does this program require, what kinds of courses would be suitable for an interdisciplinary LC, and what types of institutional supports are required? Future research will be needed to address all three of these questions, but my own study suggests that none of these obstacles is insurmountable.

Although interdisciplinary LCs have often been the province of honors programs, prior academic achievement does not appear to predict student success in an LC. Jean Mach, Michael Burke, and Jeremy Ball (2008) argue that at their two-year college, their LC provides a powerful learning experience for students, students with more varied levels of academic preparation than the Interdisc students. Future research may determine that the interdisciplinary LC model of FYC proves particularly effective or challenging with certain groups of students, but current research indicates that LC pedagogy is broadly applicable.

Would the interdisciplinary LC model work with the "wider" (Kelly 1996) interdisciplinarity required in a course combining, say, philosophy and chemistry or literature and mathematics? This question, too, requires further research. However, if the goal of the interdisciplinary LC approach to FYC is to help students recognize the rhetorical domain of disciplinary expertise through the process of making connections and comparisons, what matters most is not how seamlessly these disciplines can be integrated but the types of connections instructors—in their capacities as agents and handlers—can help students see and sell.

The question of institutional support proves the greatest obstacle to replicability and scale. Some challenges face any interdisciplinary LC. For instance, the logistics of registration regularly undermine interdisciplinary LCs; any institution committed to promoting learning communities (with or without FYC) must actively address the challenges of enrolling students into linked courses. Additionally, this study indicates the importance of having instructors attend each other's classes on a regular basis and talk with each other in front of students. Such conversations play a key role in making the epistemological domains of disciplines visible to students. Many faculty—particularly those who shoulder heavy teaching loads or strenuous research expectations—cannot afford to attend each other's classes unless program administration compensates instructors for that time.

Incorporating first-year writing instruction into an interdisciplinary LC requires additional support for both instructors and students. Instructors may benefit from the ability to work with the same instructor team more than once. That team should have a series of meetings with a writing-across-the-curriculum (WAC) professional, before and during the semester, to discuss the ways in which assignments not only immerse students in the work of the disciplines but also help make the connections between those disciplines visible. Some institutions may be able to "apprentice" an instructor to an LC (either through a course reduction or a stipend)—allowing the instructor to observe and participate in an LC before actually teaching in one.

Students might benefit from access to a writing center staffed with tutors prepared to ask questions about what students are learning about the rhetorical domains of disciplinary expertise. At other institutions, students might register for a one-credit course to discuss and write about the connections emerging in their LC. Some institutions may be able to support writing and learning in the interdisciplinary LC by assigning an undergraduate writing fellow to the LC. This fellow would not attend all class sessions of the LC but could play an important role for both students (asking questions in conferences about connections between assignments, serving as a sounding board for students articulating connections) and instructors (offering insights from those conversations with students). Whatever the mechanisms of support, it is clear that if responsibility for writing instruction is moved from a dedicated FYC component to an interdisciplinary LC, both students and instructors will require extensive and ongoing support from writing program administrators (WPAs), writing center tutors, and other individuals responsible for helping instructors assign and coach writing.

Finally, I must acknowledge that the interdisciplinary LC model of first-year writing instruction will be difficult to build in a program that relies on the labor of graduate students and part-time and contingent faculty. LCs benefit from the stability of long-term pairings, a stability that is difficult to achieve in an economy driven by short-term contracts and fluctuating student enrollments. Perhaps this research will offer a new approach to achieving a long-established goal of WPAs: building a body of empirical evidence to argue for the stable employment and professional development of part-time and contingent faculty. The institutional reality of contingent faculty could be seen as a death-knell for the interdisciplinary LC approach to FYC; alternately, this study (and subsequent studies, if they demonstrate the value of interdisciplinary LCs for student learning, retention, and the like) might help WPAs argue for a more stable instructional staff.

The interdisciplinary LC model of first-year composition would be a radical departure for most FYC programs. What this model offers, though, is a form of professional development and invigoration for faculty, a source of intellectual challenge and community for students, and an innovative response to a fundamental obstacle facing most offerings of FYC. By integrating writing instruction into an interdisciplinary learning community, the LC approach not only immerses students into disciplinary contexts that can provide meaning and exigence for genres but also scaffolds students' abilities to articulate and compare the expectations for writing across those contexts.

Stand-Alone First-Year Composition Courses

This research also has significant implications for more traditional versions of first-year composition. Although stand-alone FYC courses cannot offer students a comparative view of disciplinary ways of knowing and writing, they can realistically work toward two other goals. The concept of agents of integration suggests a first goal: to help students to understand their rhetorical situation as agents— seeking to transfer not only their writing-related knowledge but other knowledge, ways of knowing, identities, and goals as well. Helping students understand transfer as a rhetorical act means helping them recognize the institutional structures that make it necessary (and difficult) to see and sell connections. The finding that genre knowledge is a protean cognitive construct for students suggests a second important goal: getting students to question how the genre knowledge they already possess might apply or need to be reconstructed in order to provide an optimal framework for their work in other classes.

To achieve these goals, a series of reflective assignments might be woven into traditional FYC courses. The assignments would encourage students to think about the connections they see and to understand genre knowledge as a flexible construct that might be applied but might also be reconstructed. This approach focuses less on acquisition of particular antecedent genres and more on helping students articulate their own taxonomies of writing—and, importantly, on helping students see that conventions are linked to purposes and categories can be fluid. These reflective assignments might include some or all of the following:

- *At the start of the semester.* Have students (a) make a list of the types of writing they do (out of school as well as in) and (b) describe some examples of each type of writing. Instructors

could collate this information from a particular class (or group
of classes) and then ask students to complete one of the following assignments. After looking at the types of writing described
by others,

    o Compare your taxonomy to those of two or three
    classmates *or*

    o Identify and analyze trends in categories (what
    assignment types occur most often; what variation in
    names, conventions, purposes exist within categories; and
    the like)

The goal of this two-part assignment would be to help students
articulate the types of writing they are accustomed to composing and provide them with a larger framework that makes
their choices appear less inevitable, more bound to particular
contexts and experiences—and therefore more open to revision
and repurposing.

- *In the middle of the semester.* The innovative work of Jack Mino
(2006) provides one possible model of an assignment to help
students recognize their work as agents of integration in a stand-
alone FYC course: the "link aloud." The procedures of a link
aloud, as Mino describes them, are relatively simple: he asks
students to choose a paper and then read it aloud,

    paragraph by paragraph, discussing what, where, and
    how they made connections between the subject matters.
    I [use] their . . . specific word choices, operative phrases,
    interpretations, etc., to probe and sometimes provoke the
    student's thinking, particularly as it related to integration
    of material. In closing, I as[k] the students to consider
    what if any "new knowledge" or understanding did they
    discover, uncover, or construct as a result of doing this
    assignment.

FYC instructors might schedule conferences during which
they ask students to bring a paper (written for FYC or for another class) and "link out loud" about the connections between
FYC, writing they've done in the past, and writing required
in other courses.

- *At the end of the semester.* Ask students to place papers from this semester into the taxonomy articulated at the start of the semester—encouraging them to add and revise categories. Of particular interest and value are assignments that don't fit neatly into a student's taxonomy. The goal of this assignment would be to help students apply their articulated genre knowledge when possible and to begin to reconstruct that knowledge—to repurpose it and engage in the type of bricolage described in chapter 4—when necessary.

These metareflective assignments might be particularly well suited to the "writing about writing" approach to FYC articulated by Downs and Wardle (2007). But they could also be woven into a wide range of FYC offerings. These could be briefer, less-formal, reflective assignments or could become the centerpiece of an FYC curriculum.

Whatever role such assignments play in the FYC sequence, FYC instructors will benefit from an ability to clearly articulate their own taxonomy of written genres—as well as a recognition that students can productively articulate taxonomies very different from an instructor's. All writers—however experienced or inexperienced—have their own categories of writing. For agents of integration, there is no "right" taxonomy; instead, writers benefit from the ability to describe and possibly revise their taxonomy. In addition, instructors working to help students succeed as agents of integration will need a robust sense of the institutional obstacles facing students (in their capacity as agents) and instructors (in their multiple roles as agent, handler, and/or audience). In class discussions, conferences, and paper comments, instructors need to be able to illuminate for students the institutional constraints within which agents of integration see and sell connections.

Finally, instructors working to help student writers become successful agents of integration must be prepared to help students interrogate their language for talking about writing. For example, instructors might help students critically evaluate what the language of "thesis" (or, to take a different example, "rhetorical situation") enables writers to see and do—and what that terminology obscures. This research affirms the findings of many earlier studies: students can expect no common, stable vocabulary for talking about writing as they move from one context to another. Often there is only the illusion of communication, with significant differences plastered over by an ostensibly "shared" vocabulary. Agents of integration must learn to ask questions of their teachers (and other audiences) and to analyze those answers with a healthy skepticism; they must recognize that students and instructors *all* operate within institutional constraints that make it difficult to see and value connections across disciplinary boundaries. In the absence of an institutional structure (like an interdisciplinary LC) that can immerse FYC students into disciplinary inquiries and exigencies, stand-alone FYC courses can and should aim to help students develop rich vocabularies for talking about their own experiences of writing and interpreting the descriptions and expectations of others.

IMPLICATIONS FOR WRITING CENTERS

The problem of transfer is a central preoccupation in writing center work—and has most often been framed as a question of tutor expertise. However, the debate over the transferability of generalist or specialist *tutor* knowledge (see, for instance, Hubbuch 1988 and Kiedaisch and Dinitz 1993) has obscured another transfer-related challenge in the writing center: many *student writers* are struggling to become agents of integration able to transfer their own writing-related knowledge.

Acknowledging student writers as agents of integration enriches current formulations of the problem of transfer in the writing center; it does so by foregrounding the fact that tutors can simultaneously occupy two different roles. Tutors can be handlers: this is perhaps their central charge, working to facilitate the transfer of writing-related knowledge for student writers. But tutors can also be agents in their own right—developing, through their work in the writing center, a greater capacity to see and sell connections in their own writing. Recognizing tutors' two roles, as well as the difficulties facing student writers, helps to articulate several challenges for writing center work and tutor education, as well as an underappreciated contribution of writing centers to the undergraduate curriculum.

Student writers working to succeed as agents of integration need conversational partners who can help them see connections and make strategic decisions about whether and how to sell them. Writing center tutors can be these partners. Although conversations about transfer would likely *not* become central to most conferences, many writers might benefit from occasional conversations with a peer tutor playing the role of handler, asking writers to make connections and engage in the type of not talk described in chapter 4. In relatively straightforward cases of transfer-as-application, a tutor's role might be to help authors articulate and apply their already existing genre knowledge: a sociology student might find that the ways of articulating a thesis and organizing an introductory paragraph in sociology match the goals and expectations he or she associated with literary analysis. Other instances will require authors to engage in a process of transfer-as-reconstruction: a student in a clinical psychology class, for instance, might contemplate the ways in which the genre of the social science literature review differs from the book reviews he or she learned to write for the school newspaper. In other cases, tutors might help students like Betty articulate the ways in which her self-defined identity is in conflict with the identity implied by the assignment. In doing so, tutors would be engaging in the type of work advocated by Anis Bawarshi and Stephanie Pelkowski (1999), helping students "become critically conscious of how and why academic discourses construct various subject positions" (87–88). Conscious awareness of these various connections is not necessary for transfer but may make more options visible to students navigating challenging rhetorical terrain. Over time, such conversations might help agents of integration become more intentional in the connections they see and sell.

But this is a tall order for tutors. How can writing center administrators prepare tutors, whose knowledge and education are inevitably limited, to work effectively as handlers? There are at least two related challenges: First, tutors have limited knowledge of disciplines. Second, it can be difficult to know, in the real-time unfolding of a conference, when a writer is struggling as an agent of integration and how to help.

It is well established that tutors cannot possibly have rich content knowledge relevant to most papers they encounter. Content knowledge might be necessary if the tutor was trying to make the connections *for* the writer, but it is not necessary for a tutor working as a handler. Instead, my research suggests that one possible avenue to help tutors cross disciplinary boundaries is to have them interrogate and further develop their *genre* knowledge, recognizing it as a dynamic cognitive construct, the place where authors are likely to be working out the relationships among content, mechanics, and larger epistemological purposes. (This suggestion resonates with Bradley Hughes's [2002] work on the "expert outsider" knowledge of experienced tutors; he argues that expert tutors draw on knowledge of a limited number of disciplinary genres as they work across disciplinary boundaries.)

In essence, tutor education programs might prepare tutors to be effective handlers by helping them develop their own understanding of genres and disciplinary ways of knowing. As argued in chapter 3, the challenge facing many college writers is the shift from subjects to disciplines, from idiosyncrasy to epistemology. This is true of the student writers coming to the writing center, but it is also likely to be true of the student writers who become tutors. Consequently, the work of helping tutors to become effective handlers may also help tutors become more effective agents in their own writing.

To scaffold such learning, tutors might conduct inquiries into the ways of knowing and writing valued in different disciplines.

- In a cohort of tutors drawn from a range of different disciplines, each tutor might compose a "disciplinary snapshot"—in the form of a paper, a presentation, or a website—to share with other tutors. The fundamental goal would be to explain the knowledge domains, ways of knowing, and goals of their discipline or profession to fellow tutors—and in the process to transform knowledge of a subject into knowledge of a discipline. This assignment might include analysis of a prior writing assignment the tutor feels embodies one approach to writing in this discipline.
- If the tutors themselves do not represent a broad array of disciplinary backgrounds, each tutor might interview an instructor

on campus about a writing assignment: the goals of the assignment, how it fits into the goals of the course, what qualities the instructor looks for in a successful paper, and what problems the instructor frequently encounters in less-successful papers. A crucial second stage for either approach would include a meta-analysis of the tutors' research. Such meta-analysis might ask students to read their classmates' papers and "code" them. Tutors might be asked to put the assignments into categories, then explain why they categorized the assignments as they did; they could then recategorize and explain the recategorizations as many times as seemed instructive. When forced to draw up new categories for a third or fourth time, tutors may begin to see connections that they had not seen earlier and recognize the types of "ways of doing" that Michael Carter (2007) argues illuminate the rhetorical domains of disciplines.

Even possessed of such knowledge, tutors will also need to cultivate the ability to recognize moments in a conference when they might helpfully tap into that knowledge. Expert tutors are skilled in the art of conversation, most especially in the art of listening. Writing center administrators committed to helping tutors develop as handlers will have to seek ways to help tutors learn—through practice conversations and through slower-paced, finer-grained analysis of transcripts and/or videotapes of conferences—to recognize the moments when student writers are groping to make a connection but struggling to see or sell it.

Engaging in this kind of study—developing these sensitivities to what is said and unsaid, cultivating a metacognitive awareness of disciplinary genres—will not prepare tutors to respond confidently and effectively to *all* the writing assignments they will encounter. But such education will better equip tutors to help student writers articulate their own relevant genre knowledge—making the tutor a more able handler. And such education may help some tutors develop as agents of integration themselves. This is a consequence of no small importance. Peer tutors are themselves students and—as research emerging from the Peer Writing Tutor Alumni Research Project (Hughes, Gillespie, and Kail, 2010) argues—their work in the writing center is not only a service to others but also a potentially transformative educational experience for the tutor. A promising question for future research might explore the degree to which working as a writing center tutor—reading assignments and drafts and talking with writers from a wide range of classrooms and disciplines—offers students a uniquely powerful opportunity to become more successful agents of integration.

DIRECTIONS FOR FUTURE RESEARCH

I conclude by identifying four areas for future research.
- *Additional studies of rich "synchronous" slices of student learning.* This book conceptualizes students as agents of integration and argues for understanding transfer as an act of individual cognition situated in a complex social, institutional context. However, a truly robust understanding of transfer will require additional studies conducted in different contexts to revise and refine this framework.
  - o *Studies of different student populations.* I have argued that students make more connections than instructors recognize. That clearly seems true of the students enrolled in Interdisc, but what of different populations of students? The honors students in the Interdisc classroom were a relatively homogenous and privileged group. They had a history of academic success and were perhaps likely to feel authorized to write and make connections. Future studies might ask if other student populations draw the same number of connections and might trace the strategies they use when confronted with contexts that challenge their ability to see and sell connections.
  - o *Studies of the role of teacher identities in an interdisciplinary LC.* The analyses in chapter 3 convince me that the challenges Olivia faced in the interdisciplinary-gadfly mode were compounded by her identity as a feminist, a woman who was an academic generation younger than her co-instructors, and a non-Catholic. Perhaps these identifications made it riskier for Olivia to challenge traditional structures of disciplinary

authority because students saw it as a "feminist agenda" (a critique implicit in their talk of "bias" and "agenda"). Perhaps that antifeminist rhetoric was simply the most convenient, but not the most accurate, way for students to express their discontent with a pedagogy that disoriented them. This study is not positioned to answer those questions—but it does make clear the need to take up those questions in future research.

○ *Studies of different types of learning communities.* The Interdisc students—enrolled at a predominantly white, Catholic, residential college—were studying Western civilizations; many reported having studied these texts in previous classes. The texts were challenging, but they were also familiar and highly valued. Future studies might examine the effects of changing the disciplinary content of the learning community. To what extent might a student's ability to see and sell connections rely on a familiarity with the material? Or are students more likely to draw connections when faced with unfamiliar or threatening material? And what of learning communities that ask students to engage in "wide" (Kelly 1996) interdisciplinarity, linking very different disciplines?

• *Further inquiry into the types of genre knowledge that students bring into FYC classes and elsewhere.* Within Interdisc, the two most commonly referenced genres were the research paper and the analysis essay. Do these two genres wield such power for other students? Can the ubiquity of certain genres be attributed to certain stages of a student's cognitive development? To institutional structures (like advanced-placement exams and state or federal mandates)? To some combination of these or other factors? What types of writing have students done—and what kinds of writing-related knowledge do they draw on as they face new academic tasks?

• *Studies that investigate students' strategies for selling connections.* Are there particular strategies that students rely on to sell connections across disciplinary boundaries? Do certain strategies prove more or less successful? Future research might look at the strategies of student writers in a variety of contexts—FYC and beyond. They might also follow the lead of Debra Journet (1993, 1995, 1999) and Betty Samraj and John M. Swales (2000), who work to identify the "rhetoric of interdisciplinarity" in published interdisciplinary scholarship. Perhaps these published interdisciplinary writings will yield a taxonomy that can be used by students and instructors teaching for transfer.

- *Studies of the role of reflection and meta-awareness.* Finally, this research suggests the need—and a method—for future research into the role of meta-awareness in genre knowledge acquisition and transfer. My study suggests that conscious awareness of the rhetorical dimensions of genre is not necessary for transfer—but it is helpful. The transfer matrix presented in chapter 2 provides a framework to guide data collection and analysis. Future research might explore the circumstances in which awareness of seeing and selling becomes important for agents, whether those acts are linked, and how they might be cultivated.

This last question also indicates the need for comparative studies. This study was not comparative, but an obvious question for future research is the relative merits of stand-alone FYC courses, linked courses, and the interdisciplinary LC model of FYC described in this book.

Ultimately, the framework developed and the arguments advanced in this book are grounded in a deeply engaged study of a single classroom. They are bound, therefore, to show their limitations as these concepts are exported to other contexts and used for different purposes.

I am hopeful, though, that the vocabulary provided by the agents of integration framework—of seeing and selling; of agents, handlers, and audience members; of the transfer matrix; of genre as an exigence for transfer; and of genre knowledge as a dynamic cognitive construct—will continue to provide a framework not only for future research but also for the efforts of students and instructors working together to become agents of integration.

APPENDIX

REFERENCES

INDEX

APPENDIX: ASSIGNMENTS FROM THE INTERDISC SEQUENCE

History Assignments
Historical Creativity: A Medieval Diary

Assume a specific medieval identity in terms of gender, age, social position, and occupation, and write a diary entry for a single day.

First describe who you are in a sentence. Then write a diary entry for that person. Your entry should include what you do and where you do it, including physical surroundings, tools, who else is present, etc. It can be a normal day or a special day. You can simply narrate your day or, if you wish, cast the particulars in terms of your own thoughts, reactions to what is around you, etc. To the extent that you choose to discuss your thoughts and feelings, they should be thoughts and feelings appropriate to your identity and age. Note that your "day" may be the culmination of what came before or a prelude to what you expect will come later. Aim for about three pages.

Historical Criticism: Reaction Papers

At best you should direct your paper to answering the following three questions; be sure to consider the book as a whole as well as interesting segments:

1. What is the major thesis or theme of the book?

2. What is the principal insight *you* received from reading the book?

3. What questions did the book leave you with?

As a rule, "interesting thoughts" are more valuable than curious details for 2 and 3. You may address each question separately, or, better, write a single, cohesive essay.

Historical Research: Term Paper on the French Revolution

The purpose of the history term paper is to "write history" from original sources—those found in the document collection on the French Revolution edited by Baker as well as others you may uncover. The textbook will provide an overview for background and a start-up bibliography; you should also look at secondary sources as needed. Remember, however, that the essence of your paper should rely on the primary sources.

Your completed paper should not merely narrate an event but provide an analysis of a question you pose for yourself. At best, it will argue to a conclusion, a thesis.

The paper should be approximately ten to fifteen pages with appropriate documentation and bibliography, written clearly and thoughtfully. Appropriate documentation and a bibliography should make clear to the reader what ideas are yours, what ideas originated with someone else. Most important, it should be the result of an ongoing project over a number of weeks; this is not a weekend assignment. Believe me, the difference will show!

Literature Assignments

Paper 1

Below are two pairs of critical comments, one on the *General Prologue* and one on *The Wife of Bath's Prologue*. Choose *one* pair, and in a two-page paper explain which position you find more satisfactory. Your response should contain two elements (not necessarily in equal proportion): (1) Base your evaluation on your reading of a particular passage from the appropriate prologue, comparing the interpretation of Chaucer each position enables you to make; (2) you must both describe and explain the difference between the two comments.

Here's the difference, for our purposes, between describing and explaining: you describe the difference in what is said; you explain the difference in the (unspoken) assumptions underlying what is said. Ask yourself what you would have to believe in order to take each position, in order for it to be possible to say such a thing.

Paper 2

This two- to three-page paper, due Mon 2/16, asks you to make an argument about the "low" scenes (the scenes involving servants, rustics, etc.) in *Doctor Faustus*. Possible starting points: How do they relate to the rest of the play? How do you read their tone? What are the social implications of the way these low-ranking characters function in the play? What do they reveal about the model of power/knowledge/virtue/etc. operating in the play, and how does this relate to power in other texts of the course (from any of the three disciplines)?

Please remember to:

—follow Lanham's revising guidelines

—advance an argumentative thesis

—use as at least part of your evidence direct analysis of
   language from the play

Moreover:

1. Please read chapters 3 and 4 of Lanham for Wednesday.

2. As a way to weed out "paramedic" problems (excess words, passive voice, past tense, pileups of prepositional phrases, and other manifestations of distance from God), I'm asking each of you to *have a partner edit at least two paragraphs of this paper.* Please turn in to me, together with your completed draft, the draft your partner marked up *and signed* (so I know who edited whom).

Paper 3

For this four- to six-page paper about *The Merchant of Venice,* due March 31, you may choose your own topic, although I give some suggestions below.

Suggested topics:

1. Compare the relationships between gender and power in *Salve Deus* and *Merchant.* (Possible starting points: is power gendered—that is, are there separate paradigms of masculine and feminine power? Can women have power? If so, does this power come through or in spite of their femininity?)

2. Is *Merchant* supportive or critical of emergent capitalist values?

3. Compare the process of discovering truth in *Merchant* and one or more of our natural-philosophical texts (Bacon, Descartes, Harvey, Vesalius).

4. In act 1, scene 2, Portia and Nerissa differ in their evaluations of the late Duke of Belmont's will: Portia complains about him imposing his will posthumously, but Nerissa argues that he was wise and benevolent. Does the play as a whole support Portia's or Nerissa's contention?

5. What does the game the will sets up have to do with the rest of the play?

* * * *

If some of you prefer to write a paper after Easter recess, you may write about *Paradise Lost* (on its own or in conjunction with other texts), in which case the paper is due April 14.

Suggested topics:

1. Compare the versions of marriage in *Merchant* and *Paradise Lost*.

2. In book 3, God declares of Adam, "I made him just and right, / Sufficient to have stood, though free to fall" (98–99). Does the text suggest *Eve* to be equally "sufficient to stand"?

Related assignments:

1. Please read chapter 6 of *Revising Prose* for Monday 3/30.

2. As with assignment 2, you need to have a partner check/ edit at least part of an earlier draft. This time, however, you choose what you want your partner to do: "paramedic" sentence-level revising, checking a full-sentence outline, or something else. Partner should sign off, and writer should clarify for me what the task was. Partners and writers: no paramedic problems please!

Religious Studies Assignments

Paper 1

The ability to think the thoughts of another person, to put oneself in the shoes of another individual, is a skill of incomparable value both personally and professionally. It expands the horizons of the mind, combats parochialism, promotes toleration, and, in Interdisc, makes the professors happy. We have spent a good deal of time reading and discussing Aquinas. His thought is complex. His manner of arguing is difficult. His worldview is often alien. In your paper, I want you to re-create the way in which, according to Aquinas, human beings achieve salvation. You will probably want to deal with issues like virtue and habit, grace, original sin, will, free choice, predestination, etc. Since Aquinas was a nut for detail, I want you to be also. There are many little steps involved, and if one overlooks them, one loses the sense and flavor of the process. I want you to make a case for the reasonableness of Aquinas's theology on this issue. Be his defense lawyer. To do this well you will have to persuade yourself first. If you do not accept Aquinas's arguments, practice a "willing suspension of disbelief" for the period it takes to understand and appreciate Aquinas's argument. Anticipate objections to the theory, and defend Aquinas against them. You should also describe what you feel to be the operative principles or problems around which Aquinas organizes his theology on this issue. What apparently irreconcilable "truths" is he trying to harmonize?

Since some of you will in fact be unwilling to accept Aquinas's explanations, at the end you may append your own personal critique as to its failings. What key preconceptions, conclusions, or arguments separate you from Aquinas? Try to be as clear in the formulation of your own positions or objections as Aquinas is in his.

Paper 2

You have doubtless been warned about making "value judgments." It is a dangerous self-indulgence to judge the world either on the basis of unexamined prejudice or without first making a real effort to understand the objects upon which one passes sentence. Nonetheless, one cannot nor should one wish to avoid judging the value of ideas, actions, and/or means. To be totally "objective" (if it were indeed possible) would be inhuman, ignoble, and inanimate. Decisions are based on values, important decisions on important values. But to claim the respect due "values," one's opinions, biases, prejudices, and preferences must be articulated and evaluated.

Terms like *good, bad, corrupt, free, individualistic, enlightened, superstitious, unfair, immoral,* and *holy,* which often make appearances in student papers (though, of course, not in honors) are usually signs that such evaluation and articulation have not been performed. They have the unmistakable aura of gut reactions. The students who use these terms have stopped where they should have begun. "Instinctive" acceptance or rejection of ideas should trigger a process in which examination of the object is paired with reflection on the standards by which we judge that object.

With Hobbes and Locke, we have moved into a new era in religious and intellectual history. Compare one or both (you may wish to concentrate on one while making references to the other) to the preceding tradition (i.e., Anselm, Aquinas, Luther, and Calvin). What is new about their approach to religion in general and Christianity in particular? What do they reject, challenge, or reinterpret? What basic assumptions and values distinguish them from their predecessors? If they are more "modern," what is "modern" about them? What are the advantages and disadvantages of their innovations? What larger conclusions can we draw from the new approach to human and divine reality that they introduce? In general, is Christianity and/or the Western world the better or worse for what they taught? Why?

Final Exam

A major premise of Interdisc II contends that significant shifts occur in many aspects of Western culture between the ninth and eighteenth centuries. This oral exam, which you will undertake in groups of three, asks you to analyze an aspect of this transition that you find particularly interesting by comparing two clusters of material that you select from different parts of the course.

Each cluster should comprise one text from Theology, one text from Literature, and one text, development, or institution from History. You should select texts that, as a cluster, show significant similarities in light of your topic. You should select two clusters for the contrast they illustrate.

You will present your thesis for around ten minutes. We then will ask you questions, both about and departing from your presentations. In other words, we will bring up a broad range of course topics and materials for you to discuss. You are welcome to bring in photocopied passages to discuss in detail as evidence for your claims. (You may choose to use such passages during the question/answer part of the exam if you want to undertake a more extended analysis and/or for briefer references in your initial presentation.)

We will evaluate your exam on the basis of: clarity, rigor, and significance of your thesis; use of evidence to support your claims; synthesis of materials from different disciplines; rigor and depth you can bring to bear in answering questions about your thesis and clusters; rigor, depth, and breadth you can bring to bear in answering questions that range away from your thesis to other course concepts, materials, etc.

REFERENCES

AAC&U (Association of American Colleges and Universities) and Carnegie Foundation. 2004. "A Statement on Integrative Learning." Association of American Colleges and Universities and the Carnegie Foundation for the Advancement of Teaching. http://www.aacu.org/integrative_learning/pdfs/ILP_Statement.pdf.

Applebee, Arthur N., Robert Burroughs, and Anita Stevens. 2000. "Creating Continuity and Coherence in High School Literature Curricula." *Research in the Teaching of English* 34: 396–429.

Aristotle. 1991. *On Rhetoric: A Theory of Civic Discourse*. Translated by G. A. Kennedy. Oxford: Oxford University Press.

Austin, J. L. 1962. *How to Do Things with Words*. Oxford: Clarendon.

Bakhtin, Mikhail M. 1981. *The Dialogic Imagination*. Translated by Caryl Emerson and Michael Holquist. Austin: University of Texas Press.

———. 1986. *Speech Genres and Other Late Essays*. Translated by V. W. McGee. Austin: University of Texas Press.

Bauer, Dale. 1990. "The Other 'F' Word: The Feminist in the Classroom." *College English* 52 (4): 385–96.

Bawarshi, Anis. 2003. *Genre and the Invention of the Writer: Reconsidering the Place of Invention in Composition*. Logan: Utah State University Press.

Bawarshi, Anis, and Mary Jo Reiff. 2010. *Genre: An Introduction to History, Theory, Research, and Pedagogy*. West Lafayette, IN: Parlor.

Bawarshi, Anis, and Stephanie Pelkowski. 1999. "Postcolonialism and the Idea of a Writing Center." *Writing Center Journal* 19 (2): 41–58. Reprint, 2008, *The St. Martin's Sourcebook for Writing Tutors*, 3rd ed., edited by Christina Murphy and Steve Sherwood, 79–95. Boston: Bedford/St. Martin's. Citations are to the Bedford edition.

Bazerman, Charles. 1988. *Shaping Written Knowledge: The Genre and Activity of the Experimental Article in Science*. Madison: University of Wisconsin Press.

———. 1997. "The Life of Genre, the Life in the Classroom." In *Genre and Writing: Issues, Arguments, Alternatives*, edited by Wendy Bishop and Hans Ostrom, 19–26. Portsmouth, NH: Boynton/Cook.

———. 2002. "Genre and Identity: Citizenship in the Age of the Internet and the Age of Global Capitalism." In *The Rhetoric and Ideology of Genre: Strategies for Stability and Change*, edited by Richard M. Coe, Lorelei Lingard, and Tatiana Teslenko, 13–37. Cresskill, NJ: Hampton.

Beaufort, Anne. 1999. *Writing in the Real World: Making the Transition from School to Work*. New York: Teachers College Press.

———. 2007. *College Writing and Beyond: A New Framework for University Writing Instruction*. Logan: Utah State University Press.

Bender, Thomas. 1993. *Intellect and Public Life: Essays on the Social History of Academic Intellectuals in the United States*. Baltimore: Johns Hopkins University Press.

Bergmann, Linda S., and Janet Zepernick. 2007. "Disciplinarity and Transfer: Students' Perceptions of Learning to Write." *WPA* 31 (1–2): 124–49.

Boix-Mansilla, Veronica. 2005. "Assessing Student Work at Disciplinary Crossroads." *Change* 37 (1): 14–21.

Bok, Derek. 2006. *Our Underachieving Colleges: A Candid Look at How Much Students Learn and Why They Should Be Learning More*. Princeton, NJ: Princeton University Press.

Brooke, Robert. 1987. "Underlife and Writing Instruction." *College Composition and Communication* 38 (2): 141–53.

Carroll, Lee Ann. 2002. *Rehearsing New Roles: How College Students Develop as Writers*. Carbondale: Southern Illinois University Press.

Carter, Michael. 2007. "Ways of Knowing, Doing, and Writing in the Disciplines." *College Composition and Communication* 58 (3): 385–418.

Casanave, Christine Pearson. 2002. *Writing Games: Multicultural Case Studies of Academic Literacy Practices in Higher Education*. Mahwah, NJ: Erlbaum.

Chase, William G., and Herbert A. Simon. 1973. "Perception in Chess." *Cognitive Psychology* 4: 55–81.

Chi, M. T. H., P. J. Feltovich, and R. Glaser. 1981. "Categorization and Representation of Physical Problems by Experts and Novices." *Cognitive Science* 5: 121–52.

Chi, M. T. H., R. Glaser, and E. Rees. 1982. "Expertise in Problem Solving." In *Advances in the Psychology of Human Intelligence*, edited by R. J. Sternberg, 7–75. Vol. 1. Hillsdale, NJ: Erlbaum.

Chiseri-Strater, Elizabeth. 1991. *Academic Literacies: The Public and Private Discourse of University Students*. Portsmouth, NH: Boynton/Cook.

Detterman, Douglas K. 1993. "The Case for the Prosecution: Transfer as an Epiphenomenon." In *Transfer on Trial: Intelligence, Cognition, and Construction*, 1–24. Edited by Detterman and Richard J. Sternberg. Norwood, NJ: Ablex.

Devitt, Amy. 2004. *Writing Genres*. Carbondale: Southern Illinois University Press.

———. 2009. "Teaching Critical Genre Awareness." In *Genre in a Changing World*, edited by Charles Bazerman, Adair Bonini, and Débora Figueiredo, 337–51. Fort Collins, CO: WAC Clearinghouse. Available at http://wac.colostate.edu/books/genre/.

Dias, Patrick. 2000. "Writing Classrooms as Activity Systems." In *Transitions: Writing in Academic and Workplace Settings*, edited by Dias, Anthony Pare, and Marcia Farr, 11–30. Cresskill, NJ: Hampton.

Dinitz, Sue, Jack Drake, Shirley Gedeon, Jean Kiedaisch, and Char Mehrtens. 1997. "The Odd Couples: Interdisciplinary Team Teaching." *Language and Learning Across the Disciplines* 2 (2): 29–42.

Downs, Doug, and Elizabeth Wardle. 2007. "Teaching about Writing, Righting Misconceptions: (Re)envisioning 'First-year Composition' as 'Introduction to Writing Studies.'" *College Composition and Communication* 58 (4): 552–84.

Engeström, Yrjo. 1987. "Learning by Expanding." XMCA Research Paper Archive, XMCA Discussion Forum, Mind, Culture, Activity Homepage, Spring 2001. Accessed January 3, 2006. http://lchc.ucsd.edu/MCA/Paper/Engestrom/expanding/toc.htm.

Freedman, Aviva. 1993. "Show and Tell? The Role of Explicit Teaching in the Learning of New Genres." *Research in the Teaching of English* 27 (3): 222–51.

Geisler, Cheryl. 1994. "Literacy and Expertise in the Academy." *Language and Learning across the Disciplines* 1: 35–57.

Gick, M. L., and K. J. Holyoak. 1980. "Analogical Problem Solving." *Cognitive Psychology* 12: 306–55.

———. 1987. "The Cognitive Basis of Knowledge Transfer." In *Transfer of Learning: Contemporary Research and Applications*, edited by Stephen M. Cormier and Joseph D. Hagman, 9–47. San Diego: Academic.

Giltrow, Janet. 2002. "Meta-Genre." In *The Rhetoric and Ideology of Genre: Strategies for Stability and Change*, edited by Richard M. Coe, Lorelei Lingard, and Tatiana Teslenko, 187–205. Cresskill, NJ: Hampton.

Graff, Gerald. 2003. *Clueless in Academe: How Schooling Obscures the Life of the Mind*. New Haven: Yale University Press.

Gross, Neil. 2008. *Richard Rorty: The Making of an American Philosopher*. Chicago: University of Chicago Press.

Grossman, Pamela, Samuel Wineburg, and Stephen Woolworth. 2001. "Toward a Theory of Teacher Community." *Teachers College Record* 103 (6): 942–1012.

Herrington, Anne J., and Marcia Curtis. 2000. *Persons in Process: Four Stories of Writing and Personal Development in College*. Urbana, IL: National Council of Teachers of English.

Hubbuch, Susan M. 1988. "A Tutor Needs to Know the Subject Matter to Help a Student with a Paper: ____ agree____disagree____not sure." *Writing Center Journal* 8 (2): 23–30.

Huber, Mary Taylor, and Pat Hutchings. 2005. *Integrative Learning: Mapping the Terrain*. Washington, DC: Association of American Colleges and Universities.

Huber, Mary Taylor, Pat Hutchings, Richard Gale, Ross Miller, and Molly Breen. 2007. "Leading Initiatives for Integrative Learning." *Liberal Education* 93 (2): 46–51.

Hughes, Bradley. 2002. "The Wisdom of 'Expert Outsiders': Genre Knowledge Possessed by Experienced Writing Center Tutors." Paper presented at the annual meeting of the International Writing Centers Association Conference, Savannah, GA.

Hughes, Bradley, Paula Gillespie, and Harvey Kail. 2010. "What They Take with Them: Findings from the Peer Writing Tutor Alumni Research Project." *Writing Center Journal* 30 (2): 12–46.

Jamieson, Kathleen M. 1975. "Antecedent Genre as Rhetorical Constraint." *Quarterly Journal of Speech* 61: 406–15.

Journet, Debra. 1993. "Interdisciplinary Discourse and 'Boundary Rhetoric': The Case of S. E. Jelliffe." *Written Communication* 10 (4): 510–41.

———.1995. "Synthesizing Disciplinary Narratives: George Gaylord Simpson's *Tempo and Mode in Evolution*." *Social Epistemology* 9: 113–50.

———. 1999. "Writing within (and between) Disciplinary Genres: The 'Adaptive Landscape' as a Case Study in Interdisciplinary Rhetoric." In *Post-process Theory: Beyond the Writing-process Paradigm*, edited by Thomas Kent, 96–115. Carbondale: Southern Illinois University Press.

Kelly, James S. 1996. "Wide and Narrow Interdisciplinarity." *JGE: The Journal of General Education* 45 (2): 95–113.

Kiedaisch, Jean, and Sue Dinitz. 1993. "Look Back and Say 'So What': The Limitations of the Generalist Tutor." *Writing Center Journal* 14 (1): 63–74.

Leskes, Andrea. 2005. Foreword to *Integrative Learning: Mapping the Terrain*, iv–v. Edited by Mary Huber and Pat Hutchings. Washington, DC: Association of American Colleges and Universities.

Mach, Jean, Michael Burke, and Jeremy Ball. 2008. "Integrative Learning: A Room with a View." *Peer Review* 10 (4): 20–23.

McCarthy, Lucille P. 1987. "A Stranger in Strange Lands: A College Student Writing across the Curriculum." *Research in the Teaching of English* 21 (3): 233–65.

Miller, Carolyn. 1984. "Genre as Social Action." *Quarterly Journal of Speech* 70: 151–67.

Mino, Jack. 2006, August. "The Link Aloud: Making Interdisciplinary Learning Visible and Audible." Learning Communities. Accessed September 26, 2009. http://www.cfkeep.org/html/snapshot.php?id=6508959910375.

Nelms, Gerald, and Rhonda L. Dively. 2007. "Perceived Roadblocks to Transferring Knowledge from First-year Composition to Writing-intensive Major Courses: A Pilot Study." *WPA* 31 (1–2): 214–40.

Nowacek, Rebecca S. 2005a. "A Discourse-Based Theory of Interdisciplinary Connections." *JGE: The Journal of General Education* 54 (3): 171–95.

———. 2005b. "Negotiating Individual Religious Identity and Institutional Religious Culture." In *Negotiating Religious Faith in the Composition Classroom*, edited by Elizabeth Vander Lei and Bonnie I. Kyburz, 155–66. Portsmouth, NH: Boynton/Cook.

———. 2007. "Toward a Theory of Interdisciplinary Connections: A Classroom Study of Talk and Text." *Research in the Teaching of English* 41 (4): 368–401.

———. 2009. "Why Is Being Interdisciplinary So Very Hard to Do? Thoughts on the Perils and Promise of Interdisciplinary Pedagogy." *College Composition and Communication* 60 (3): 493–516.

Perkins, David N., and Gavriel Salomon. 1988, September. "Teaching for Transfer." *Educational Leadership* 46 (1): 22–32.

———. 1989, January–February. "Are Cognitive Skills Context-Bound?" *Educational Researcher* 18 (1): 16–25.

Polya, George. 1957. *How to Solve It: A New Aspect of Mathematical Method.* 2nd ed. Garden City, NY: Doubleday.

Reiff, Mary Jo, and Anis Bawarshi. Forthcoming. "Tracing Discursive Resources: How Students Use Prior Genre Knowledge to Negotiate New Writing Contexts in First-Year Composition." *Written Communication.*

Russell, David R. 1995. "Activity Theory and Its Implications for Writing Instruction." In *Reconceiving Writing, Rethinking Writing Instruction*, edited by Joseph Petraglia, 51–78. Mahwah, NJ: Erlbaum.

———. 1997. "Rethinking Genre in School and Society: An Activity Theory Analysis." *Written Communication* 14: 504–54.

Russell, David R., and Arturo Yañez. 2003. "'Big Picture People Rarely Become Historians': Genre Systems and the Contradictions of General Education." In *Writing Selves/Writing Societies: Research from Activity Perspectives*, edited by Charles Bazerman and Russell, 331–62. WAC Clearinghouse. http://wac.colostate.edu/books/selves_societies/.

Samraj, Betty, and John M. Swales. 2000. "Writing in Conservation Biology: Search for an Interdisciplinary Rhetoric." *Language and Learning across the Disciplines* 3 (3): 36–56.

Schryer, Catherine F. 1994. "The Lab vs. the Clinic: Sites of Competing Genres." In *Genre and the New Rhetoric*, edited by Aviva Freedman and Peter Medway, 105–24. London: Taylor and Francis.

Schunk, Dale H. 2004. *Learning Theories: An Educational Perspective*. 4th ed. Upper Saddle River, NJ: Pearson.

Searle, J. R. 1969. *Speech Acts: An Essay in the Philosophy of Language*. Cambridge: Cambridge University Press.

Smit, David W. 2004. *The End of Composition Studies*. Carbondale: Southern Illinois University Press.

Sternglass, Marilyn. 1997. *Time to Know Them: A Longitudinal Study of Writing and Learning at the College Level*. Mahwah, NJ: Erlbaum.

Strauss, Anselm. 1987. *Qualitative Analysis for Social Scientists*. Cambridge: Cambridge University Press.

Tannen, Deborah. 1994. *Gender and Discourse*. New York: Oxford University Press.

Tardy, Christine M. 2009. *Building Genre Knowledge*. West Lafayette, IN: Parlor.

Thaiss, Chris. 2001. "Theory in WAC: Where Have We Been, Where Are We Going." In *WAC for the New Millennium: Strategies for Continuing Writing Across the Curriculum Programs*, edited by Susan H. McLeod et al., 299–326. Urbana, IL: National Council of Teachers of English.

Thaiss, Chris, and Terry Myers Zawacki. 2006. *Engaged Writers and Dynamic Disciplines: Research on the Academic Writing Life*. Portsmouth, NH: Boynton.

Walvoord, Barbara E., and Lucille P. McCarthy. 1990. *Thinking and Writing in College: A Naturalistic Study of Students in Four Disciplines*. Urbana, IL: National Council of Teachers of English.

Wardle, Elizabeth A. 2004, July 27. "Can Cross-Disciplinary Links Help Us Teach 'Academic Discourse' in FYC?" *Across the Disciplines* 2. Accessed April 15, 2009. http://wac.colostate.edu/atd/articles/wardle2004/index.cfm.

———. 2007. "Understanding 'Transfer' as Generalization from FYC: Preliminary Results of a Longitudinal Study." *WPA* 31 (1–2): 65–85.

———. 2009. "'Mutt Genres' and the Goal of FYC: Can We Help Students Write the Genres of the University?" *College Composition and Communication* 60 (4): 765–89.

Yancey, Kathleen Blake. 1992. "Teacher's Stories: Notes toward a Portfolio Pedagogy." In *Portfolios in the Writing Classroom*, edited by Kathleen Blake Yancey, 12–19. Urbana, IL: National Council of Teachers of English.

———. 1996. "Portfolio as Genre, Rhetoric as Reflection: Situating Selves, Literacies, and Knowledge." *WPA* 19 (3): 55–69.

Zawacki, Terry Myers, and Ashley Taliaferro Williams. 2001. "Is It Still WAC? Writing within Interdisciplinary Learning Communities." In *WAC for the New Millennium: Strategies for Continuing Writing Across the Curriculum Programs*, edited by Susan H. McLeod, Eric Miraglia, Margot Soven, and Christopher Thaiss, 109–40. Urbana, IL: National Council of Teachers of English.

INDEX

Rebecca S. Nowacek is an associate professor of English and directs the writing center at Marquette University. She has published essays in *College Composition and Communication*, *College English*, *Research in the Teaching of English*, and *JGE: The Journal of General Education*. She was also a scholar with the Carnegie Foundation's CASTL Program and a coeditor (with Michael B. Smith and Jeffrey L. Bernstein) of *Citizenship across the Curriculum*.

CCCC STUDIES IN WRITING & RHETORIC

Edited by Joseph Harris, Duke University

The aim of the CCCC Studies in Writing & Rhetoric (SWR) series is to influence how writing gets taught at the college level. The methods of studies vary from the critical to historical to linguistic to ethnographic, and their authors draw on work in various fields that inform composition—including rhetoric, communication, education, discourse analysis, psychology, cultural studies, and literature. Their focuses are similarly diverse—ranging from individual writers and teachers to classrooms and communities and curricula, to analyses of the social, political, and material contexts of writing and its teaching. Still, all SWR volumes try in some way to inform the practice of writing students, teachers, or administrators. Their approach is synthetic, their style concise and pointed. Complete manuscripts run from 40,000 to 50,000 words, or about 150–200 pages. Authors should imagine their work in the hands of writing teachers, as well as on library shelves.

SWR was one of the first scholarly book series to focus on the teaching of writing. It was established in 1980 by the Conference on College Composition and Communication (CCCC) to promote research in the emerging field of writing studies. Since its inception, the series has been copublished by Southern Illinois University Press. As the field has grown, the research sponsored by SWR has continued to articulate the commitment of CCCC to supporting the work of writing teachers as reflective practitioners and intellectuals. For a list of previous SWR books, see the SWR link on the SIU Press website at www.siupress.com.

We are eager to identify influential work in writing and rhetoric as it emerges. We thus ask authors to send us project proposals that clearly situate their work in the field and show how they aim to redirect our ongoing conversations about writing and its teaching. Proposals should include an overview of the project, a brief annotated table of contents, and a sample chapter. They should not exceed 10,000 words.

To submit a proposal or to contact the series editor, please go to http://uwp.aas.duke.edu/cccc/swr/.

OTHER BOOKS IN THE CCCC STUDIES IN WRITING & RHETORIC SERIES